The Cambridge Introduction to
Harriet Beecher Stowe

Through the publication of her bestseller *Uncle Tom's Cabin*, Harriet Beecher Stowe became one of the most internationally famous and important authors in nineteenth-century America. Today, her reputation is more complex, and *Uncle Tom's Cabin* has been debated and analyzed in many different ways. This book provides a summary of Stowe's life and her long career as a professional author, as well as an overview of her writings in several different genres. Synthesizing scholarship from a range of perspectives, the book positions Stowe's work within the larger framework of nineteenth-century culture and attitudes about race, slavery and the role of women in society. Sarah Robbins also offers reading suggestions for further study. This introduction provides students of Stowe with a richly informed and accessible introduction to this fascinating author.

Sarah Robbins is Professor of English at Kennesaw State University, Georgia.

Cambridge Introductions to Literature

This series is designed to introduce students to key topics and authors. Accessible and lively, these introductions will also appeal to readers who want to broaden their understanding of the books and authors they enjoy.

- Ideal for students, teachers, and lecturers
- Concise, yet packed with essential information
- Key suggestions for further reading

Titles in this series:

Eric Bulson *The Cambridge Introduction to James Joyce*

John Xiros Cooper *The Cambridge Introduction to T. S. Eliot*

Kirk Curnutt *The Cambridge Introduction to F. Scott Fitzgerald*

Janette Dillon *The Cambridge Introduction to Early English Theatre*

Janette Dillon *The Cambridge Introduction to Shakespeare's Tragedies*

Jane Goldman *The Cambridge Introduction to Virginia Woolf*

Kevin J. Hayes *The Cambridge Introduction to Herman Melville*

David Holdeman *The Cambridge Introduction to W. B. Yeats*

M. Jimmie Killingsworth *The Cambridge Introduction to Walt Whitman*

Rónán McDonald *The Cambridge Introduction to Samuel Beckett*

Wendy Martin *The Cambridge Introduction to Emily Dickinson*

Peter Messent *The Cambridge Introduction to Mark Twain*

John Peters *The Cambridge Introduction to Joseph Conrad*

Sarah Robbins *The Cambridge Introduction to Harriet Beecher Stowe*

Martin Scofield *The Cambridge Introduction to the American Short Story*

Emma Smith *The Cambridge Introduction to Shakespeare*

Peter Thomson *The Cambridge Introduction to English Theatre, 1660–1900*

Janet Todd *The Cambridge Introduction to Jane Austen*

Jennifer Wallace *The Cambridge Introduction to Tragedy*

The Cambridge Introduction to
Harriet Beecher Stowe

SARAH ROBBINS

CAMBRIDGE
UNIVERSITY PRESS

CAMBRIDGE UNIVERSITY PRESS
Cambridge, New York, Melbourne, Madrid, Cape Town, Singapore, São Paulo

Cambridge University Press
The Edinburgh Building, Cambridge CB2 2RU, UK

Published in the United States of America by Cambridge University Press, New York

www.cambridge.org
Information on this title: www.cambridge.org/9780521671538

First published 2007

Printed in the United Kingdom at the University Press, Cambridge

A catalogue record for this publication is available from the British Library

Library of Congress Cataloguing in Publication data

Robbins, Sarah.
The Cambridge introduction to Harriet Beecher Stowe / by Sarah R. Robbins.
   p.   cm. – (Cambridge introductions to literature)
Includes bibliographical references.
ISBN-13: 978-0-521-85544-0 (hardback)
ISBN-10: 0-521-85544-6 (hardback)
ISBN-13: 978-0-521-67153-8 (pbk.)
ISBN-10: 0-521-67153-1 (pbk.)
1. Stowe, Harriet Beecher, 1811–1896 – Criticism and interpretation.   I. Title.   II. Series.
PS2957.C38   2007
813′.3 – dc22

ISBN 978-0-521-85544-0 hardback

ISBN 978-0-521-67153-8 paperback

Contents

Preface

Harriet Beecher Stowe is a familiar name to students of literature and history. However, many of the details we "know" about her and about her most famous book, *Uncle Tom's Cabin*, are based more in myth than in her actual life. One of the goals of this book is to peel back the sometimes contradictory elements of that mythology. Another is to position her work within the context of her own day, while also acknowledging the major critical controversies that have swarmed around her since then.

Although Stowe was a major figure in American and world literary culture throughout the second half of the nineteenth century, she faded from view through much of the twentieth. Feminist scholarship re-ignited interest in Stowe in the 1970s, and research on her life and writing has expanded a good deal since then. Questions about the literary value of her publications and about her personal attitudes on race continue to puzzle general readers and academics, however. And these questions provide one major rationale for studying Stowe today.

Acquiring a clear sense of Stowe's life, her writing, and its place in literary history can be challenging, given the wide range of opinions about her. This book will serve as a basic introduction to such topics. The "Life" chapter offers a biographical overview. "Cultural Contexts" provides a survey of significant issues and trends shaping Stowe's career. The "Works" chapter explores her major publications. Because *Uncle Tom's Cabin* continues to claim the most intense critical attention, and because it was so significant a force in Stowe's own time, much of the "Works" chapter concentrates on that text and Stowe's related anti-slavery writing (*A Key to Uncle Tom's Cabin*; *Dred: A Tale of the Great Dismal Swamp*; and *The Christian Slave*). Other writings are much more briefly introduced, including examples of her regionalist fiction, her travel writing, and her social satire. The overview for each of Stowe's major works includes a concise treatment of the plot, themes, and major characters, with some explanation of key topics recurring in criticism. The "Reception" chapter outlines ways that various groups of readers, influential critics, and other literary artists have responded to Stowe, particularly to *Uncle Tom's Cabin*. Learning about the controversies surrounding *Uncle Tom's Cabin* – and their links to literary history – is crucial, since so much of what we see of her today is the product of many divergent responses to her first novel.

For an extensive biographical treatment and analysis of how Stowe's life was shaped by the culture of her lifetime, readers can consult Joan Hedrick's prize-winning 1994 biography, *Harriet Beecher Stowe: A Life.* Those who would like to learn more about Stowe's individual publications can consult *The Cambridge Companion to Harriet Beecher Stowe* (ed. Cindy Weinstein) and the list of secondary criticism at the end of this volume.

Acknowledgments

Many generous colleagues have contributed to this book. Susan Belasco recommended I take on the project in the first place – providing a strong vote of confidence for an otherwise very daunting task. Student research assistant Louise Sherwood carried source-seeking to a new level. Kennesaw State University's Interlibrary Loan staff provided unflagging assistance securing materials, and the Bentley Special Collections librarians found just the right cover art. While I was drafting, students in several courses provided insightful feedback.

Special thanks to colleagues who read sections of the manuscript. Debra Rosenthal checked multiple chapters, sending thoughtful suggestions via email from England. LeeAnn Lands, Catherine Lewis, and Ann Pullen gave careful input on historical analysis. Anne Richards, Laura McGrath, and Katarina Gephardt provided timely readings of core chapters. Kimberly Wallace-Sanders and Mark Sanders gave encouraging and enlightening feedback on my discussion of *Uncle Tom's Cabin*, the responses of various audiences, and the history of criticism.

Ray Ryan, Elizabeth Davey and Maartje Scheltens at Cambridge were supportive guides throughout the project's many stages.

Families of literary historians have to be patient when long-dead writers come to live with us, taking up physical space with books and papers, but also claiming time and energy. Harriet Beecher Stowe can be a particularly insistent presence. I am lucky to have a husband (John) and two daughters (Margaret and Patty) who have been kind enough to let her stay around for so long.

Abbreviations

The abbreviations below are used for frequently cited sources within both the text and endnotes.

Agnes	*Agnes of Sorrento*
Cambridge Companion to HBS	*The Cambridge Companion to Harriet Beecher Stowe*, edited by Cindy Weinstein
Dred	*Dred: A Tale of the Great Dismal Swamp*
HBS	*Harriet Beecher Stowe: A Life*, by Joan D. Hedrick
Key	*A Key to Uncle Tom's Cabin*
Life	*Life of Harriet Beecher Stowe, Compiled from Her Letters and Journals*, by Charles Stowe
Life and Letters	*Life and Letters of Harriet Beecher Stowe*, edited by Annie Fields
PL	*Palmetto Leaves*
PW	*Pink and White Tyranny*
SM	*Sunny Memories of Foreign Lands*
"UL"	"Uncle Lot"
UTC	*Uncle Tom's Cabin*

Chapter 1

Life

Harriet Beecher Stowe's life mirrored that of many other white, middle-class women of her generation. But her highly productive writing career set her apart in a number of ways. While other nineteenth-century American women authors like Catharine Maria Sedgwick, Fanny Fern (Sara Parton) and Frances Harper also had notable success, Stowe was unusual in the range of genres she helped shape and in her ability to call upon diverse resources to support her work. Many of her professional opportunities derived from her family connections, which mitigated gender-based constraints faced by other women of her day.

Beecher lore and community vision

Stowe's Beecher family lineage had a significant impact on the way her contemporaries perceived her. During her lifetime, family members and friends worked hard to create an image that would appeal to her reading audience. During her declining years, her son Charles Stowe wrote the first authorized biography, where he cast *Uncle Tom's Cabin* as "a work of religion" guided by the same republican principles that had motivated the Declaration of Independence and "made Jefferson, Hamilton, Washington, and Patrick Henry anti-slavery men."[1] Around the same time, Florine Thayer McCray, a Hartford neighbor, prepared another biography. McCray built her book to a rousing conclusion celebrating "the noble legacy" of Stowe's writings and "the priceless heritage of her personal example."[2] Close friend Annie Fields published *Life and Letters of Harriet Beecher Stowe* in 1897, just after Stowe's death, reinforcing the message that the author's career had been unselfishly dedicated to the anti-slavery cause. The cumulative power of such texts initiated a meaning-making *process* distinctive from the actual historical person Harriet Beecher Stowe. Therefore, we need to recognize that much of what we think we know about her – such as the anecdote Annie Fields told about Abraham Lincoln's crediting Stowe with starting the Civil War – is strategic lore that should be read critically.[3] However saintly the initial guardians of her heritage painted her, Stowe's life was more complex than the legends they promoted.

This collaborative enterprise of representing "Harriet Beecher Stowe" in an array of nineteenth-century texts was also supported by the author's own astute management of her career. Though her reputation would always remain tied to her major bestseller, *Uncle Tom's Cabin*, she capitalized on that milestone with later writing in a range of genres, while helping to shape the development of American literature. Overall, she was unique in her time for the breadth and influence of her work as an American woman writer.

At the heart of her success was a vision of New England life as a stand-in for an idealized America. This view of Protestant, middle-class New England as representing the best of republican values would permeate her writing, even in those moments when her satirical pen highlighted its flaws. In drawing on imagined versions of a moral social order, Stowe tapped into a tradition beginning as far back as the founding of New England in the 1600s. In the colonial era, Puritan settlers saw their new home as an extension of England but also as a special domain of God's chosen people. Over time, progressing toward a new republic, the highly literate, middle-class leaders of New England maintained their ties with the home country (for example, in choosing place names) but also formed a distinctive American identity organized around their regional culture. Thus, "creating New England, that is, imaginatively drawing the boundaries of regional identity, involved an ongoing process of cultural negotiation."[4] In the nineteenth century, Stowe's Beecher family members contributed to this agenda through social activism and self-conscious cultural production.

Stowe's own unending search for an ideal community, grounded in deep religious principles but also in a recognition of human frailties, would shape her life choices as well as her writing. In family moves to antebellum Cincinnati, her multiple journeys to Europe, the Stowes' extended trips to Florida, and her "model housekeeping" designs for homes back in New England, we can see a parallel to Stowe's literary imaginings of utopian communities. Meanwhile, even as she drew on increasingly varied contacts with cultures different from her native region, these moves into new geographic and psychic spaces did not ever dislodge her deep-seated ties to a traditional vision of American social virtue.

A Beecher education for social agency

From the outset, Harriet Beecher Stowe's upbringing envisioned possibilities for cultural influence both enabled and constrained by her gender. Born in 1811, she grew up in Litchfield, Connecticut, where her father worked as a Congregational minister. The seventh child of Roxana Foote Beecher and Lyman Beecher, Harriet came into a family that set high expectations for all its children. Yet, conscious of the limitations she would face as a woman, Lyman Beecher is reported to have said early on that he wished Harriet had been born a boy, since she showed signs already of being able to outshine her brothers.

Young Harriet attended an unusually progressive school, the Litchfield Academy. She excelled in John Brace's composition class, her favorite. When she won a writing contest and had her work read aloud at a school exposition, she was excited to see her father's intent interest in her text – even before she had been identified as the author. If Lyman Beecher's rapt listening marked the writing as worthwhile, Harriet would declare in a memoir years later, she knew she had achieved a meaningful accomplishment.

At age 13, Harriet became a boarder at the Hartford Female Seminary, then led by her eldest sister Catharine. The younger sister quickly moved from student to assistant teacher. Even though Harriet's later success as the author of *Uncle Tom's Cabin* has obscured this period in her professional development, it is important to recognize the connections between her literary arguments for women's social influence and this early experience.

Later, during Catharine's long absence for a rest cure, Harriet served as head administrator. In exploring ideas about female learning through collaboration with other young women attending the seminary, Harriet Beecher came up with a governance plan less hierarchical than her sister had used. Harriet's was a system based on collaborative "circles" for team management. Her letters to Catharine during this period reflect the younger sister's enthusiasm for teaching, but also for institution-building.[5] Reflecting on the expanding possibilities for women's education, Harriet was envisioning the first of many utopian programs that she would promote over a lifelong career as a reformer.

The reputation of the Hartford Female Seminary grew so much that it attracted bright young women from the midwest and south as well as from New England.[6] Thus, this work exposed Harriet to a broader range of social interaction than we might expect. By adding more challenging elements to the curriculum than was typical in most young women's institutions, the seminary had also earned praise from advocates for female education, including Sarah Josepha Hale. A pioneer in the field, the seminary provided an apt training ground for students – but also for the Beecher sisters themselves.[7] The one discouraging challenge impeding the institution was financial. Catharine eventually became so frustrated with supporters' inability to raise a substantial endowment that she welcomed an invitation from her father to relocate to Cincinnati, Ohio, then considered an outpost of the American west.

Navigating Cincinnati as a cultural "contact zone"

Arriving in Cincinnati in 1832, Catharine and Harriet laid out ambitious plans to open schools for children and young ladies, while their father headed up Lane Seminary. Writing to her friend Georgiana May back east, Harriet declared: "We mean to turn over the West by means of *model schools* in this, its capital" (qtd in Charles Stowe, *Life*, p. 72).

Harriet's years in Cincinnati represented a defining time in her life, since her experiences there promoted her growth as both a teacher and a writer, and later as a married woman juggling domestic activities with authorship aspirations. In the antebellum era, Cincinnati represented many of the possibilities associated with a thriving American culture. Though less refined than New England, the city was attracting numerous settlers from the northeast, and this group aimed to transplant the values of their home region into this western crossroads.

Central to this endeavor, for those in the Beecher family's social group, was the Semicolon Club, a combination social and literary society. Stowe was at first so nervous about presenting her writing that she carried out elaborate steps to conceal her identity as author of one early sketch. Although most of the texts by the club's members were never formally published, but simply presented orally at their regular gatherings, the opportunity to have her writing shared publicly marked an important stage in Harriet Beecher's development as an author. Harriet actually captured an award for "Uncle Lot," an 1833 piece she originally wrote for the club and afterwards submitted to a contest. The prize money for this narrative sketch, which was published in James Hall's *Western Monthly Magazine*, affirmed her writerly aspirations. In addition, the vision of New England life that she achieved in her Semicolon Club sketches helped define one of the longstanding agendas for her publishing career. By the mid 1840s, in fact, she had written enough sketches to create a book-length collection, *The Mayflower.*

Despite residing in Ohio, many of the club members still viewed New England as both home and an ideal site of American culture. This stance is evident in an ornate book, *The Semicolon*, which the club published locally.[8] In one of *The Semicolon*'s sketches, for example, New England flowers carried west for replanting in the new soil there are equated with the larger political and cultural goal of refining the region.

If the Beechers and their contemporaries saw themselves as civilizers of a still-rough western region, they also found that Cincinnati was bringing them into a dynamic space of cultural diversity – what Mary Louise Pratt has called a "contact zone."[9] With the slave state of Kentucky just across the Ohio River, New England-bred residents – often for the first time in their lives – came into regular contact with slave owners and slaves. Harriet Beecher herself visited a Kentucky plantation in 1833, soaking up images she would revive years later when writing *Uncle Tom's Cabin.* Meanwhile, the slavery issue was becoming increasingly intense in Cincinnati itself. Debates raged among students at Lane Theological Seminary and, even more disturbingly, abolitionist advocates trying to work in the city were coming under direct assault. Stowe herself would write in a letter that a mob attack on the anti-slavery periodical co-published by J. G. Birney and Gamaliel Bailey was appalling enough to "'make converts to abolitionism'" among her family members (qtd in Charles Stowe, *Life*, p. 84).

In January of 1836, Harriet married the widower Calvin Stowe, a teacher at Lane Seminary. Harriet's letter to her old friend Georgiana May, written less than an hour before the ceremony, conveys some ambivalence about a marriage that would nonetheless endure: "Well, my dear, I have been dreading and dreading the time, and lying awake all last week wondering how I should live through this overwhelming crisis, and lo! It has come and I feel *nothing at all*" (qtd in Charles Stowe, *Life*, p. 76).

Though Harriet and Calvin's marriage would be a long one, successful by measures of the time, it was not without tensions. One of these revolved around Calvin's sexual needs, which played out both in his wife's many pregnancies and in Harriet's sometimes taking long vacations on her own. Another stress point arose from Calvin's penchant to criticize, on the one hand, and Beecher family members' tendency to interfere, on the other. In 1846, Harriet sought temporary escape by visiting the popular "water cure" in Brattleboro, Vermont. But she wrote to Calvin regularly while enjoying the hydrotherapy there, and she bore her sixth child, Samuel Charles, almost exactly nine months after her return to Cincinnati.

Besides her trips back east, Stowe used regular letter-writing to Georgiana May and others throughout the years in Cincinnati to maintain her strong ties with New England. Thus, even though she published relatively little during the first decade of her marriage, Stowe was an active writer, often examining large-scale social issues in her correspondence. When the time came to leave Ohio and return to New England, she was poised for more public writing addressing questions tied to the conflicts she had observed firsthand in the west.

Composing *Uncle Tom's Cabin* while housekeeping in Maine

Stowe moved to Brunswick, Maine, in April 1850, during the height of the US debates over slavery. After almost two decades working in Ohio, Calvin Stowe had accepted a call to Bowdoin College. Harriet found the task of setting up a new home quite challenging, even though she was enthusiastic about this return to her native region. Calvin had been left behind in Cincinnati, where he had one more term of teaching at Lane Seminary. In letters and periodical pieces, Harriet used imagery calculated to portray herself as an isolated, even beleaguered, domestic manager. Yet she was on the verge of beginning her most famous publication, *Uncle Tom's Cabin*.

Stowe and her fellow family members had been appalled by passage of the Fugitive Slave Law. The new legislation required northerners to return any escapee to slavery, so those who had positioned themselves as anti-slavery but who had resisted full-fledged abolitionism were suddenly in a quandary. Before, they could distance themselves from the sins of slaveholders; now, if confronted with a runaway, they must either break the law or have their own morality sullied by following its dictates. For Stowe, passage of this act was a turning point. Stowe's father, Lyman Beecher, had earlier opposed efforts by students at Lane Seminary to take an active stand for abolition, and Stowe had followed his lead in assuming an anti-slavery stand short of outright abolitionism. But with encouragement from her younger brother, Henry Ward Beecher, and another brother and sister-in-law, Mr and Mrs Edward Beecher, Stowe shifted her position to a more activist stance.

However inspired she was by righteous indignation over the Fugitive Slave Law, Stowe was also quite aware that her writing could bring dollars into her family's restricted coffers. Calvin had hoped that his new salary would be adequate to their needs, but Harriet learned that housing in Bowdoin could not be had for the $75 per month he had budgeted. Committed to having her writing generate income, she rented a large house for $125, even though it clearly needed repairs.[10]

By this time, Stowe had already published in Gamaliel Bailey's *National Era*, an anti-slavery periodical. Her contributions had been sentimental stories and humorous sketches (e.g., "A Scholar's Adventures in the Country") like those she had written in Cincinnati, rather than polemical assaults on slavery. Soon after passage of the 1850 compromise legislation, however, she had submitted "The Freeman's Dream," a parable calling up a resolute Christ to condemn a farmer for failing to help a runaway slave family. Appearing in early August, this piece apparently encouraged Stowe to see the *Era* as a space where she could combine the familiar gendered modes of her earlier writing with a newly politicized voice. When Bailey sent her a generous check to encourage more submissions, Stowe determined to write a piece that would rally opposition to the new law.

Though Stowe was lucky to have an editor eager for her submissions and a publication suited to her anti-slavery goals, she was not so fortunate in having day-to-day living arrangements that would support the composition of her most ambitious narrative to date. With her husband still in Ohio, Harriet was supervising repairs on the Maine house. Feeling the stress of this assignment, along with the burdens of mothering a large brood of children, she was hardly in a position to write a novel-length narrative. Yet, she was well aware that publication was the readiest tool at her disposal for aiding the family's pressing financial situation. In this regard, the *Era*'s format, accommodating serialized installments, was a benefit. She could squeeze in snatches of time for writing between her other maternal duties, which included managing a small family school and overseeing housekeeping arrangements. Frustrating though the frequent interruptions to her writing would be – and Stowe's letters to her husband say that crying babies and household emergencies constantly intervened – she at least could spread out the narrative in manageable segments. In fact, over the course of serialization, which ran from June 1851 to April 1852, Stowe missed her deadline only three times.

The serial was so popular that it attracted new subscribers to the *Era* and encouraged Stowe to bring the narrative out in book form. Negotiations with one publisher broke down based on the firm's prediction that anti-slavery writing would not sell well. But Stowe soon found another publisher, John P. Jewett. When the first edition of *Uncle Tom's Cabin* came out in the spring of 1852, Stowe's first novel became a bestseller of unprecedented proportions. Virtually overnight, the woman who had not long ago depicted herself in a sketch for Sarah Josepha Hale's compendium of women's biographies as "retired and domestic," a "teacher" and a "mother to seven children," became a celebrity author.[11]

Traveling as an international celebrity

Once *Uncle Tom's Cabin* exploded into the American literary marketplace, it was quickly exported to Europe. With the anti-slavery movement having become increasingly popular in England, Stowe was invited by abolitionist leaders of Great Britain to visit there. In this era before international copyrights, Stowe was not reaping benefits from the many pirated editions of her book being sold overseas. But she was astute enough to realize that making direct contact with her readers in Europe could pay any number of dividends for her career. So she eagerly embarked for England in 1853, on the first of several European trips, with several family members in tow.

Stowe's determined efforts to manage the international dimensions of her publishing enterprise underscore ways in which, despite her self-depictions as a modest housewife, she was already dealing assertively with professional author-ship. Indeed, Stowe's careful self-presentation during her European travels as a humble, gentle, ladylike figure needs to be viewed with critical awareness. Clearly, she garnered social, political, and even financial rewards from such moves. For example, on her first trip to Great Britain, she secured not only a petition of support for the anti-slavery movement in the United States, but also valuable gifts that became family heirlooms. A journal her brother Charles maintained during the Stowes' first trip to England is telling. Recounting an exchange with his sister's supporters in Edinburgh in April 1853, for instance, he noted:

> Mrs. Douglas [Stowe's hostess] produced a beautiful box of
> *papier-mâché*. Inside were all ladies' working articles and a beautiful
> *agate cup* about the size of a saucer cut out of Scotch pebble, as it is
> called. A beautiful work of art, of a dark wine color. This cup was filled
> with gold pieces. There were just 100 sovereigns, which Mrs. Douglas
> said her husband had laid aside for Mrs. Stowe *herself*. The penny
> offering was for the slaves. This was for *herself*.[12]

While happily accepting such gifts and accolades from enthusiastic fans, Stowe also followed through on her goal of negotiating copyrights that pro-tected her family finances. Travel in Europe also enabled Stowe to provide her children with access to cosmopolitan society at a level beyond what she and her siblings had achieved in their youth. At one point, for instance, Stowe left her twin daughters to study in Paris. In addition, European travel inspired Stowe with new topics for her writing, including a travel book (*Sunny Memories of Foreign Lands*) and a novel set in Italy (*Agnes of Sorrento*).

Stowe's *Sunny Memories* emphasizes her enthusiasm for Europe, including an attraction to aristocracy at odds with her supposed dedication to American republican values. Still, her incorporation of Europe into her writing and her world view was guided by her New England family's background. Her pilgrimages to religious sites were complemented by visits to literary landmarks such as the home of Sir Walter Scott, a childhood favorite. Drawn to some elements of Italian culture, she sought ways to synthesize such features as veneration of the Virgin Mary with her Calvinist frame of experience. Similarly, her friendships with leading European ladies like the Duchess of Sutherland were cast not only as professional literary connections but also around values associated with female Christian virtue. Overall, as she did with other cross-cultural interactions in her life, Stowe negotiated her relationships with Europe and Europeans through the framework of her Beecher family ties.

Re-envisioning New England domesticity

Stowe's continued identification with New England as a homeplace and the professional benefits she gleaned from this affiliation are clear in the eagerness with which she returned there after each of her European sojourns. Though she often complained about the pressures of domestic management, she reveled in the ways that her writing income enabled an upgrade in the family's house when Calvin took a post at Andover Theological Seminary. In these efforts, she joined other well-to-do New England women of her generation by acquiring new household conveniences and displaying signs of her family's wealth.

Stowe capitalized on homemaking as a theme by producing magazine sketches and a book on household management, *House and Home Papers*. She became adept at getting double duty from her texts about domestic life. For instance, in 1865, she wrote a series of pieces for the *Atlantic Monthly* that were later anthologized into an expensive gift book (Hedrick, *HBS*, p. 318).

The ambivalence in Stowe's attitude toward New England housekeeping in these years can be traced in part to her family's becoming increasingly dependent on her writing for financial support. In 1863, Calvin Stowe retired from his position at Andover. Then Harriet faced even more pressure to write for immediate financial reward. Longer narratives claimed her interest intellectually, but short pieces could bring in cash more quickly. Sometimes, during this middle phase of her career, she yearned for the chance to focus on a carefully sequenced novel. Instead, she often found herself negotiating with multiple editors, seeking to put off one who was still waiting for a major project, while enticing another to accept a briefer contribution that could pay some bills right away. The need for high volume, in turn, led Stowe to encourage her unmarried twin daughters, Hatty and Eliza, to take over more day-to-day household affairs. At the same time, she was managing the education of the younger children in her large brood and dealing with her husband's ambivalent attitude toward her continued literary success.

Given the complex feelings Stowe had about her own domestic role in the decades after *Uncle Tom's Cabin*, we can see a tension between the writing in which she glorified New England home life – as in *The Minister's Wooing*, *The Pearl of Orr's Island*, and *Oldtown Folks* – and her distaste for daily running of her household. But she continued to seek an ideal model, both in her writing and in the creation of her family's own living arrangements.

In the 1860s, while the Civil War raged, Stowe supervised the building of Oakholm, a large, well-decorated house with features taken from the Italian architecture she had loved seeing in Europe. In Nook Farm, a stylish Hartford neighborhood where the Samuel Clemens (Mark Twain) family and her half-sister Isabella Beecher Hooker's clan also lived, Stowe trumpeted her professional success through domestic design. She hired the same contractor who had built Isabella and John Hooker's showplace, and she supervised every element in the construction, including the digging of drains and the architectural refinements.

In this as in other domestic enterprises, Stowe struggled to embody traditional housewifery while also sustaining a busy writing career. The tension between these goals could sometimes work to her advantage, however. She often invoked her pressing domestic duties to put off editors, while she simultaneously used her writing responsibilities to escape housekeeping chores.

The lure of the south

In 1867, Stowe traveled for the first time to an area along the St Johns River, where she and Calvin would construct a second home. Like the "snow birds" of today, for years the Stowes made regular trips back and forth between the north and south, spending summers in Hartford and winters in Mandarin, Florida.

Ever the educator and reformer, Stowe had been drawn to the idea of a southern home partly by a wish to contribute to the Reconstruction-era education of freed slaves. As early as 1866, she had written her brother Charles: "My plan of going to Florida, as it lies in my mind, is not in any sense a worldly enterprise . . . My heart is with that poor people whose course in words I have tried to plead, and who now, ignorant and docile, are just in that formative stage in which whoever seizes has them."[13] Reflecting both her commitment to blacks' post-war uplift and her continued sense of racial hierarchy, Stowe's comments foreshadowed a work to which she would give much energy – the development of a religious school for black and white children in the neighborhood where she bought a winter bungalow. In this sense, the Stowes' transplanting in Florida was similar to the Beechers' move to Cincinnati decades earlier – with both involving a cross-regional uplift mission.

Stowe was also genuinely charmed by Florida – particularly by its lush natural environment. Troublesome as the treks back and forth would be, challenging though the ongoing fund-raising for the school would become, the retreats to Florida provided a restorative combination of purposeful work and relative leisure, amid an environment of tropical beauty and domestic simplicity. From November through May over many years, Stowe and her husband really seemed to have found new peace far from New England.

Yet, there were many distractions and setbacks between Stowe's acquisition of her southern getaway and her final return to Hartford. Readers were horrified by her frank depiction of Lord Byron's purported incest in *Lady Byron Vindicated*. Not since the southern reviews of *Uncle Tom's Cabin* had she met with such wrathful responses in print. When all of America became scandalized by charges that her brother Henry Ward had seduced the wife of a parishioner, Theodore Tilton, Stowe became caught up in that controversy as well. Perhaps most painfully, the death of her daughter Georgiana, named for the beloved New England friend of her youth, brought back memories of other tragedies in her children's lives, including Henry's accidental drowning and Fred's recurring bouts with alcoholism. Amid these challenges, Stowe found a continued sense of achievement in her writing. As with her earlier European-inspired texts, Stowe's Florida sketches brim with appreciation for their subject. Meanwhile, enchanted as she was with Mandarin, she also wrote a nostalgic narrative revisiting her own New England childhood in *Poganuc People*.

Final days in Hartford

Despite Stowe's enthusiasm for Florida, when her husband's health slipped markedly in the mid-1880s, she opted to nurse him in Hartford, near her family and friends. Later, in the years after Calvin's death in 1886, Stowe's children would follow suit, tending to their mother's long mental twilight in the comfort of their hometown. Born and bred in Connecticut, Stowe ended her life there in 1896, the power of her intellect faded and the reservoir of her financial resources nearly exhausted. Stowe's reputation as an author was already waning too, as conceptions of aesthetic value had shifted dramatically over the course of the nineteenth century. It would remain for feminist critics of the next century to begin recovering her status in literary history and to draw new readers to her texts.

Cultural contexts

Stowe's eighty-five years spanned most of the nineteenth century. So, an important step toward understanding her long career is to identify cultural trends during that era. Major factors shaping Stowe's writing included shifting conceptions of middle-class American womanhood; the growth of American literature; racial politics; Protestant religious influence on US society; and efforts to build a cross-regional and transatlantic social class committed to cultural leadership.

Middle-class womanhood

One important trend in nineteenth-century American society was the separation of men's and women's responsibilities in middle-class family life, supporting belief in domesticity as women's realm of work. Whereas, in the colonial era, husbands and wives had collaborated in a predominantly rural economy to provide subsistence for their families, nineteenth-century urbanization brought with it an increasing tendency for men to work outside the home and women to be in charge of the so-called "domestic sphere." In governing that sphere, cultural arbiters such as magazine editor Sarah Hale argued, women actually exercised enormous social influence by teaching children and guiding their husbands in moral directions. Women were supposed to be particularly adept at "moral suasion," an approach for encouraging enlightened behavior that was linked to females' heightened spiritual sense.[1]

The ideology of domesticity certainly constrained women's opportunities in some ways (for example, by limiting their access to careers). But this vision of women's rightful leadership as home-based could also be empowering. Through their mandate to manage children's learning, for instance, middle-class women were molding what was often termed the "rising generation," thereby having substantial indirect influence on politics. Extending this role, women began to assert that they were the ones best suited to teach young children outside the home as well. Gradually, therefore, schoolteaching became a women's profession. In a related trend, women used the educational responsibilities assigned to them by the ideology of domesticity to obtain enhanced access to learning themselves. Whether as mothers training their sons or as schoolteachers serving the community, this argument went, women needed to be well educated themselves. Thus, the curriculum for US females gradually shifted from learning "accomplishments" needed to attract a mate to serious study in line with women's anticipated teaching duties.[2]

As dominant as the ideology of domesticity may appear to have been, it was certainly not universally available; nor was it appealing to all middle-class women. Working-class women could hardly enact a model that assumed they would spend their days at home. Indeed, the labor of servants and industrial workers (often immigrants) helped free up northern middle-class women from time-consuming chores such as food preparation, laundering, and clothes-making to devote more energy to learning, teaching, and genteel leisure. In the south, slave women carried out a similar role for mistresses, while also facing such horrific potential abuses as sexual assault by masters and the break-up of slave families. Furthermore, although the rhetoric associated with domesticity depicted the ideology as an ideal, some middle-class women actively resisted its limits – and increasingly so as the century progressed.

One watershed moment occurred in 1848. The meeting of women activists at Seneca Falls, New York, produced the Declaration of Sentiments, modeled on the Declaration of Independence to claim political rights for women. Led by Elizabeth Cady Stanton and Susan B. Anthony, the American campaign for women's rights operated on multiple fronts: publishing, convenings of women activists, and lobbying Congress to enlist male supporters. Consistent with having acquired some leadership in education, women earned the right to participate on local school boards toward the end of the century, long before they could vote in national elections.

Besides suffrage, which was not achieved on a national level until 1920, other concerns of the nineteenth-century women's movement included securing various legal rights for women in abusive marriages (like the right to divorce, the right to child custody), gaining access to additional careers (such as medicine), and, for more radical leaders, developing strategies for limiting pregnancies. Meanwhile, for African American women like Josephine Ruffin,

Frances Harper, and Ida B. Wells-Barnett, balancing a commitment to women's rights with devotion to racial uplift was challenging, especially given the racism evident among some white leaders of the women's suffrage campaign.

Although Stowe never became a radical activist in the nineteenth-century women's rights movement, she was highly engaged throughout her career by questions about women's place in American society. Interestingly, Stowe was reportedly frustrated by the constraints associated with her gender as she was growing up. When her brothers went on rough-and-tumble jaunts with her father, she felt left out. At one point, she is said to have put on a boyish black coat and cast aside her needle and thread, preferring to join in a project of gathering wood for the family hearth (Hedrick, *HBS*, 19). But this effort to take on a male role was short-lived for Harriet Beecher, who spent most of her life strategically applying the model of feminine domesticity rather than resisting it.

Stowe benefited personally from the enhanced access to learning gained by proponents of domesticity such as her sister Catharine and Sarah Hale. Stowe's teaching at the Hartford seminary, as well as her work at schools in Ohio and Florida, grew out of her own opportunities to study a curriculum that would have been inaccessible to many in her mother's generation. For most of her adult life, in fact, Stowe was operating some type of school – often managing home-based lessons for her own and neighbors' children. Stowe also made strategic use of domestic ideology's belief in moral suasion. For instance, several white middle-class mother figures in *Uncle Tom's Cabin*, such as Mrs Bird and Rachel Halliday, exercise authority through sentimental techniques associated with that framework.

Even though Stowe's younger half-sister Isabella Beecher Hooker would become a vocal leader in the women's rights movement, the oldest Beecher sister, Catharine, was adamant in her opposition to women's suffrage. Harriet generally positioned herself somewhere in between Isabella and Catharine. Stowe was clearly uncomfortable with the most extreme leaders of the post-Civil War era, particularly the infamous Victoria Woodhull. Woodhull, the first woman to run for US president, faced several scandals about her personal life. Though Isabella was a staunch defender, Harriet created a wicked caricature of Woodhull in *My Wife and I*, where Audacia Dangyereyes's off-putting behaviors critique Woodhull and those of her ilk.

Still, Stowe herself could be roused to a more proactive position when unfair assaults on women's morality came into play. Her defense of Lady Byron (*Lady Byron Vindicated*) offered a gendered argument against the abuses her friend had suffered through Lord Byron's profligate behavior. Critics' furious attacks on her treatment of the Byron story may seem surprising, since exposure of

Lord Byron's sins was in line with the mandate for middle-class women to serve as guardians of morality. Unfortunately, in this case Stowe ran head on into a more powerful expectation: that a proper middle-class woman would remain aloof from the darkest elements of society, even if that meant covering them up. Earlier in her career, Stowe had come under similar fire for acknowledging in *Uncle Tom's Cabin* that women slaves faced sexual abuse at the hands of their masters. In both of these cases, we can see her commitment to safeguarding women's personal morality, even though she was not ready to lead the charge for suffrage.

Writing American literature

In the decades after the Revolutionary War, American leaders began to distance US from British literature. This effort was part of a larger post-colonial movement to establish a distinctive American culture, independent of the mother country. Creating a national literature was, in some ways, a daunting enterprise. Economically, the lack of an international copyright through much of the nineteenth century meant that it was typically cheaper to buy pirated editions of English literature than to purchase an American-authored book. Culturally, questions were repeatedly raised about the new nation's ability to generate literary texts worthy of serious readership. Along those lines, in a famously dismissive editorial published in the *Edinburgh Review* in 1820, Sidney Smith asked: "In the four corners of the globe, who reads an American book?"[3] In fact, for many decades in the US, British authors outsold American ones.

As the century unfolded, though, American writers claimed a growing readership. Authors like James Fenimore Cooper (in his Leatherstocking series), Lydia Maria Child (in *Hobomok* and stories for her juvenile magazine) and Catharine Maria Sedgwick (in books like *Hope Leslie*) often grounded their narratives in America's own past. Poets like William Cullen Bryant and Henry Wadsworth Longfellow took advantage of the grandeur of the American landscape as a literary subject. The literary era sometimes dubbed the American Renaissance emerged in the decades before the Civil War.

By mid-century, some early signs of the eventual divide between high art and literature with a broader appeal were becoming apparent. One dividing line developed around gender. In a trend that would reach fuller articulation at the turn into the twentieth century, serious-minded publications such as *Putnam's Magazine* (founded in 1853) called for a distinction between rigorously conceived American literature by artistically oriented male authors and sentimental "trash" being circulated by women writers. In one 1855 editorial, for instance, *Putnam's* lambasted American women writers for their lack of "artistic impulse," their emphasis on "pecuniary reward" (i.e., making money from their writing), and their "stereotyped flux of sentiment." Associating female writing with excessive emotion, the editorial exalted an alternative, masculine model that "treat[ed] national subjects like a man" to create a "national and vigorous" literature.[4] Conflating sentimental writing with women's writing, discussions like these began erasing links between this body of literature – admittedly placing a high premium on appealing to readers' feelings – and a serious tradition of writing based on late eighteenth-century male English models of sensibility. Reducing the sentimental – and by extension women's writing – to tears-making, this stance would have lasting effects on American literature, promoting high/low divisions based on gender.

Part of the anxiety about women's writing evident in the *Putnam's* editorials can be traced to the frustration some literary men were feeling over women's rise in the publishing marketplace. Women readers were crucial to the development of a national literature, and women writers aimed to address the desires of those readers. Whether in the seduction-and-fall novels Cathy Davidson examines from the early national period or the mature-and-find-a-husband story Nina Baym identifies from women's fiction between 1820 and 1870, American women writers understood that having middle-class women situated within the domestic sphere guaranteed a large group of readers with an interest in female-oriented topics.[5] And these women readers and writers also helped ensure the popularity of sentimentalism as a literary mode.

Nathaniel Hawthorne grumbled about the "damned mob of scribbling women" dominating the marketplace, but the men turned things around toward the end of the nineteenth century and early in the twentieth when writer-critics like T. S. Eliot, William Dean Howells, and Henry James successfully narrowed conceptions of "the literary" in American culture. With an increasing stress on high-art craft, distanced point of view, and tightly structured designs that became crucial to modernist and New Critical visions of literary value, nineteenth-century women writers would fade from view, especially in academic circles.

Somewhat ironically, women like Fanny Fern (Sara Parton) had helped professionalize American authorship in the first place by demonstrating that writing could actually generate substantial income. Vital to that development was the rise of lending libraries and the periodical press, which provided affordable access to texts for more readers and, at the same time, a potentially profitable venue for writers. Nineteenth-century newspapers and magazines blended reportage with fictive texts in ways that have fallen out of favor today, as publications like the *New Yorker*, *Harper's*, and the *Atlantic* have become more the

exception than the rule in the US. However, throughout Stowe's career, periodicals for middle-class readers regularly mixed multiple genres – partly based on
a much broader concept of what constituted "the literary" than we have now.
Blending numerous modes of writing, these periodicals helped authors make
a living from their work. For instance, serializing novels in magazines was a
common practice, enabling writers to collect income from that first round of
publication before earning more from a subsequent book version.

On a parallel track with periodicals for middle-class readers, cheap publications for the working classes came on the scene, especially in the urban northeast. Improving rates of literacy and increasing capacities for print production
and circulation all combined to foster this trend. Story papers (inexpensive
weeklies printing multiple serials in each issue), pamphlet novels (free-standing
novelettes of around 50–100 pages), and, beginning around 1875, "cheap
libraries" were all often lumped together under the term "dime novels."[6] Some
of these publications recounted wild-west adventures, while others depicted
dark, corrupt city life or told detective stories. Often aimed at urban workmen,
dime novels would be carried off to battle by Civil War soldiers, but also tucked
in the pockets of servant women. Some gentry-class cultural arbiters worried
over the publications' potential to corrupt simple-minded lower-class readers,
but others saw this expanding market as an opportunity for uplift – leading to
publications with overtly reformative goals. In any case, this was a broad field
for money-making by authors and publishers.

Stowe was actively involved in all the major trends driving the growth of the
literary marketplace in her day. In *Uncle Tom's Cabin*, we can recognize how
well her writing was positioned to succeed in American literary culture. For one
thing, her narrative clearly announced itself as a national story: she addressed
the most volatile political issue of the antebellum era, thereby drawing her
countrymen to her text, while also encouraging European readers to see her
novel as a window into a divided American society. For another, by basing her
appeal to readers in techniques of sentimentalism, she unabashedly positioned
her novel in a tradition of gendered literature. Frequently speaking directly to
readers in a motherly voice, she signaled an expectation that women would be
her main audience, whether on their own or as directors of a family's parlor
reading. Writing initially for serialization in the *National Era* periodical, she
showed little concern for honing narrative structure, concentrating instead on
spinning out her episodes with a combination of melodrama and moral appeal
consistent with that publishing venue and with readers' loose conceptions of
literary genre in her day. Once *Uncle Tom's Cabin* was published in book form,
it was re-packaged in formats for working-class readers, both at home and
abroad. Indeed, one measure of the novel's success was its unusual ability to

appeal to readers across class lines, in forms ranging from the most expensive of leather-bound, illustrated gift volumes to the cheapest of dime novel-type abridgements.

In the final stages of her career, Stowe tried to balance money-making goals for her writing with concerns about her literary legacy. She would take advantage of her fame as the author of the century's most stunning bestseller to attract readers to later publications. Some of these – such as the compendium of biographies in *Men of Our Times* (1868) – seem more pragmatically calculated than artistically conceived. She would be especially productive in the periodical venue, both as a contributor to magazines like the *Atlantic* and the *Independent*, and as an editor herself (for *Hearth and Home*).

In taking a practical approach to writing as a professional enterprise, Stowe may have weakened her position in the pantheon of nineteenth-century literature. However, amid the push for dollars, she produced memorable texts later in her career which are now drawing increased attention from critics. As this process unfolds, we may develop greater appreciation for the match between her later works' content and evolving measures of literary greatness in the final decades of the nineteenth century.

Racial politics

Race was at the center of nineteenth-century American politics. In the first half of the century, the debate over slavery dominated the national agenda. In the decades after the Civil War, the focus shifted to questions about how to incorporate newly freed African Americans into the national community – especially how to address their educational needs. In both periods, racial essentialism, a belief assigning innate traits to entire race groups, had a significant impact on Americans' thinking.

During the antebellum era, slaveholding states resisted calls for immediate or even gradual abolition, and they sought to build support for maintaining slavery as an institution by extending it into the west. Debates over allowing slavery into the territories, therefore, were both philosophical and strategic.

In their efforts to sustain the union in the face of divisions over slavery, politicians were reaping the bitter harvest of the founding fathers' failure to resolve the issue when drafting the US Constitution. For many years, however, maintaining this uneasy situation of having two Americas – slave and free – was made more likely by the fact that northerners could compartmentalize slavery as a southern problem or could even actively oppose it by assisting escapees. The Fugitive Slave Law destroyed this tenuous balance. Confronted with a runaway slave, a northerner would now be forced to break one of two laws: the secular one calling for return of the fugitive to the south or the moral one opposing slavery on humanitarian grounds.

Up until 1850, many northerners – including members of the Beecher family – would have identified themselves as anti-slavery, while stopping short of abolitionism. White abolitionists like Lydia Maria Child (an avid opponent of Indian Removal as well), William Lloyd Garrison (publisher of *The Liberator*), and the Grimké sisters (Angelina and Sarah) were definitely in the minority. Abolitionists supporting an immediate end to slavery were viewed as extremists, threatening the union.

Part of what made the continuation of slavery possible for so long was the racism that permeated northern society. Nineteenth-century science supported hierarchical views of racial identity that, in turn, bred racism. In line with ideas about evolution, racial identity was viewed as being solely biological, and some races were assumed to be inherently superior to others. In particular, antebellum science positioned the Anglo-Saxon race as advanced over the African and assigned fixed traits to each group. Whites, for example, were supposed to be naturally more assertive and capable, blacks more docile and in need of direction.

Meanwhile, the stresses of an urbanizing economy in the north brought with it competition over labor opportunities that reinforced racial tensions. As Jacqueline Jones has noted,

> The lowly immigrant canal digger determined to hold on to his sense of superiority while toiling alongside a black co-worker; the failing artisan, who saw in the black hod carrier's poverty his own future degradation; and the haughty Philadelphia merchant, dependent on his southern slaveholding customers – all of these whites believed they had much to lose in any situation where blacks had anything to gain. From these tensions arose an image of African Americans as doubly dangerous: as poor people and yet also as politically aggressive people.[7]

Discourse supporting negative stereotypes was one strategy for managing these tensions.

In the face of such challenges, free blacks in the north exercised important leadership in the abolitionist movement. Publishing slave narratives that stressed the capability of former slaves, organizing political action teams, and providing educational uplift programs were just a few of the approaches black abolitionist leaders used to build support for the cause.

Given the complex context around race relations in the antebellum era, it should not be surprising that Harriet Beecher Stowe could write a mid-century anti-slavery novel which was itself highly racist by today's standards. Furthermore, while Stowe's position on such issues as the colonization of Liberia evolved over time, in response to criticism by black leaders such as Frederick Douglass, she never developed truly collegial friendships with black Americans.

Stowe's abiding belief in the natural superiority of her own race can be linked to an associated view of her gentry class as having special gifts and therefore unique responsibilities for social benevolence. During almost twenty years in Cincinnati, just across the Ohio River from a slave state, Stowe's family did aid fugitives, and Stowe herself taught the children of escaped slaves in her own home. But, following the lead of patriarch Lyman Beecher, the family studiously avoided taking an abolitionist stance. And the Beechers were certainly not alone in their position. Many leaders of the women's suffrage movement refused to embrace abolitionism, and some were even silent on the question of slavery itself.

Not until the Fugitive Slave Law endangered the Beechers' own position as morally opposed to slavery did they shift to abolitionism. Even then, Stowe published her *Uncle Tom's Cabin* serial in the relatively moderate *National Era*, not in *The Liberator*. In her characterizations of blacks for that novel and later works, we can see stereotypes consistent with the racial essentialism of her day, such as her proposition that blacks are easily drawn to Christianity by their "natural" docility and her assigning of minstrelsy related traits to Topsy. However much Stowe identified with slave mothers suffering over the loss of their children, she may well have been more like the standoffish Miss Ophelia in her own interactions with African Americans than the loving little Eva.

Religion

For Stowe, as for the majority of nineteenth-century Americans, Protestant belief systems guided daily social practices and larger moral choices. While a number of the Founding Fathers had been Deists, envisioning a "watchmaker" God who created the Universe and then left it to operate through rational choice, in New England the tradition of Calvinism brought to America by the region's Puritan founders remained strong from the colonial era on into the nineteenth century. Calvinist thought assumed that the elect – those chosen by God – would attain a sense of their own salvation through grace rather than good deeds. Anyone who did not achieve a conviction of personal conversion was doomed to damnation. Although strict Calvinism assumed that one could not gain admission among the elect through mere personal effort, the need to embrace grace and salvation as coming freely from God encouraged intense introspection and an acceptance of humankind's innate unworthiness. At its best, therefore, Calvinism could promote deep reflection and humility.

Nineteenth-century Calvinism had several features in common with other American Protestant faiths. One was an assurance that Protestant Christianity was the best source of leaders and principles to guide the republic. Another was a related confidence in America as a blessed nation. Like the individual elected by God for salvation, the United States had a holy role to play in the world, directed by a shared Christian faith among its people.

The close relationship between Christianity and advanced civilization was another shared assumption among nineteenth-century American Protestants. Southerners actually drew on this concept to justify slavery; being a Christian- ized slave in the US was often touted as being far better than living free but heathen in Africa. Political leaders throughout the nation invoked the same basic principle of Protestant Christianity's superiority to justify such actions as Indian Removal, expansions into western territories, and warfare to gain Catholic Mexican lands. The rightful superiority of Protestant Christianity could even be called upon to manage cultural conflict within the US – with Irish Catholics, for instance.

Even though nineteenth-century Americans' Protestant religious vision could be applied in such questionable ways, it also made undeniable contribu- tions to social welfare. Among northerners, the anti-slavery campaign was often conceived and carried out in highly religious terms. The Women's Christian Temperance Union, though sometimes stereotyped today as a busy-body orga- nization, was driven by a religious impulse to protect women and children from the social problems associated with husbands' and fathers' excessive drinking – such as loss of family income and physical abuse. Similarly, though the bur- geoning home and foreign mission movements of the nineteenth century could be faulted for imposing a Christian belief system on others, Protestant mission workers in the US and abroad did provide enhanced medical care, access to literacy, and employment.

Stowe's own family background immersed her in religious culture from birth onward. Her father Lyman Beecher was a leading Congregationalist clergyman, and all of her brothers entered the ministry, with several achieving national lead- ership positions.[8] Henry Ward Beecher, a younger brother especially close to Stowe, became renowned for stirring sermons at Plymouth Church in Brook- lyn, social activism, and many religious publications.[9] Her husband Calvin Stowe, though a scholar rather than a pastor, was also an ordained minis- ter. Much of Stowe's writing represented a kind of literary ministry, since the traditional pastoral role was inaccessible due to her gender.[10]

An abiding aim of Stowe's writing was to promote the moral values of Protestant religious culture. Some of her earliest writing affiliated with the Christian temperance movement, and she published pieces in religious periodicals throughout her long career. In *Uncle Tom's Cabin*, she positioned her anti-slavery argument in a spiritual context and repeatedly addressed Christian mothers; in *A Key to Uncle Tom's Cabin* and *Dred*, she reserved some of her harshest criticism for pro-slavery church leaders' twisting of Christian principles to support a sinful institution. Her regionalist fiction on New England life placed the church at the heart of the community.

Given the negative image often associated with Calvinism today, it may be hard to imagine why Stowe's family could have been so firmly committed to its tenets. Lyman Beecher's brand of Calvinism was, in some ways, less somber than what we often associate with the faith. Personally, Stowe's father was more genial and even fun-loving than the stereotype Calvinist churchman embodied in the Jonathan Edwards of "Sinners in the Hand of an Angry God" fame. Nonetheless, Stowe and some of her siblings had cause to pull away from their father's faith. Lyman Beecher was a strict enough Calvinist to insist, when the fiancé of Stowe's sister Catharine Beecher died in a shipwreck without having achieved a conviction of personal salvation, that the young man was surely damned. Harriet was so struck by the inflexibility of this stance that she critiqued it in *The Minister's Wooing* in the reactions of Mrs Marvyn and the heroine Mary Scudder, after the apparent death of young James Marvyn at sea.

Stowe herself eventually turned away from her father's Calvinism to become Episcopalian. But even as she shifted denominations, Stowe never broke from her sense of the resources religion could provide for society. When she bought land in Florida after the Civil War, one of her first projects was to try persuading her brother Charles Beecher to establish a church there. And when she portrayed divisions between Episcopalians and Congregationalists in her late-career novel *Poganuc People*, she also emphasized their shared Christian values.

Class identity

Like most prominent Americans of their day, the Beecher family defined their personal identities in relation to others. For one thing, they positioned themselves imaginatively on a social map of the US that was responding to tensions dividing the country, thereby seeing themselves as *not* southern but northern. But their sense of themselves was also tied to their commitment to social influence, and, unlike the distancing of regional identification, this affiliative self-defining process involved embracing an identity that crossed geographic lines.

Nineteenth-century American families like the Beechers viewed themselves as members of a sub-group within the larger middle class – one dedicated to cultural leadership typically achieved less through accumulation of wealth than through careers in education, the ministry, law, and related professions. Scholars have suggested several labels for this social group, ranging from "gentry" to "Victorian intellectuals" to "Anglo-American culture-makers."[11] To maintain their strong sense of class identity in an era when so many Americans were moving to new parts of the country, members of this group defined themselves more by shared social practices than by the place where they were living at a particular time. Many of the group's leaders affiliated strongly with a New England background and, through reading, writing, travel, and religion, with some elements in English culture as well. (Hence the terms "Victorian" and "*Anglo*-American.")

Cross-regional and transatlantic cultural exchange was crucial to sustaining shared identity and to the group's various social agendas. Letter-writing, for example, could connect a former resident of Massachusetts who had moved to Michigan with friends and family back east. Providing accounts of what one was reading and thinking invited correspondents to share intellectual work. Written communications and travel – enhanced by improving transportation systems – enabled group members to collaborate on projects ranging from temperance campaigns to fundraising for home missions.

Members of this social class could bolster their gentry status with travel to Europe. Self-improvement acquired through European journeys, in turn, supported individuals' capacity for group leadership. Well before her own forays overseas, Stowe's family had already tapped into this approach for gaining cultural authority when, at the request of Ohio politicians eager to improve schooling in the west, Harriet's husband Calvin took an extended trip to Germany to study education systems. And much earlier, Stowe herself had mined the resources of English intellectual capital through study in her educated family setting. Shakespeare, Byron and Sir Walter Scott, for instance, were authors she eagerly read as supplements to the non-fiction religious works her father also recommended.

Certainly, Stowe's strong affiliation with England through such reading helped her to make the most of her travels to Europe. On each of her visits, Stowe also strengthened personal contacts with various literary and social reform leaders, such as Harriet Martineau. To sustain those connections, she could draw on her years of writing highly literary letters to family members scattered around the US. For instance, English writer George Eliot (Mary Ann

Evans) became one of Stowe's favorite correspondents, with the two authors exchanging responses to each others' work as well as social commentary on issues of the day.

Stowe's copious letter-writing to friends and family continued throughout her lifetime. By circulating information and ideas among her many correspondents, Stowe reinforced the regional, national, and international social networks that supported her personally and professionally. For instance, when writing to her son Charles as he studied in Bonn, she described her progress serializing a novel; when drafting a letter to her Boston editor, Oliver Wendall Holmes, she referenced English colleagues in reform movements (Fields, *Life and Letters*, 359–75). In this as in so many other practices, Stowe drew on cultural resources of her social class, while also exercising influence tied to the distinctive reach of her authorship.

Chapter 3

Works

Though Stowe's fame – in her lifetime and today – is inextricably linked to *Uncle Tom's Cabin*, she was actually a highly prolific author whose publications spanned over half a century. Surveying both continuities and distinctions among her many works can highlight ways in which her influence on literary culture built upon but also extended beyond her best-known text.

Early writings

Harriet Beecher Stowe began her first piece of published fiction by introducing its New England setting. In the opening paragraph of "Uncle Lot," an 1834 story originally called "A New England Sketch," she described her beloved home region both by explaining what it was *not* – a scene for literary romance – and by touting its special features:

> And so I am to write a story – but of what, and where? Shall it be radiant with the sky of Italy? Or eloquent with the beau ideal of Greece? Shall it breathe odor and languor from the orient, or chivalry from the occident? Or gayety from France? Or vigor from England? No, no; these are all too old – too romance-like – too obviously picturesque for me. No; let me turn to my own land – my own New England.[1]

Stowe's "Uncle Lot" invited her readers on an imaginative visit to the village of Newbury. She focused on several distinctive personalities, among them her title character, Uncle Lot, "a chestnut burr" of a man. She emphasized the links between his personality and his home village, which she simultaneously presented as typical of New England and, hence, an American ideal, viewed through a nostalgic if not overly romanticized lens. Uncle Lot Griswold, after all, was "abounding with briers without and with substantial goodness within. He had the strong-grained practical sense, the calculating worldly wisdom of his class of people in New England; he had, too, a kindly heart," even though sometimes "crossed by a vein of surly petulance" ("UL," p. 8). Alongside Uncle Lot, her story presented his son George, his wife Aunt Sally, and his daughter Grace. Together, they formed a unit that would be as central to Stowe's writing as her region – the family.

If Uncle Lot was the masculine version of New England's identity, Grace was a feminized ideal:

> Pretty in her person and pleasant in her ways, endowed with native self-possession and address, lively and chatty, having a mind and a will of her own, yet good-humored withal, Miss Grace was a universal favorite. It would have puzzled a city lady to understand how Grace, who never was out of Newbury in her life, knew the way to speak, and act, and behave, on all occasions, exactly as if she had been taught how.   ("UL," p. 9)

Though seeming to be "one of those wild flowers," grown up "in the woods" as if "there by nature," Grace was, in fact, a prime example of a cultivated New England upbringing. Energetic and "adept in all household concerns," she was also an eager reader, studying "whatsoever came in her way. . . . [And] what she perused she had her own thoughts upon, so that a person of information, in talking with her, would feel a constant wondering pleasure to find that she had so much more to say of this, that, and the other thing than he expected" ("UL," p. 9).

It is tempting to read Grace and Uncle Lot as stand-ins for Harriet and her father Lyman Beecher, as we can see parallels in the descriptions above. More likely, Stowe means her characters to be types, consistent with her own experience if not drawn directly from it. Still, there are signs of the Beechers' well-known confidence in the role of their social class: Stowe's young hero James Benton is first a teacher and later a minister, for instance.

The slim plot of "Uncle Lot" retraces a courtship played out on multiple levels. James Benton, the new schoolmaster, quickly captures the heart of Grace. Her father is not so easily won. But James perseveres and finds his cause aided by the return of Grace's brother George to the village, where George is set to work as a minister. When George befriends James, Lot begins to see the young schoolmaster in a more positive light, especially once the older man realizes that his son has recognized a hearty strength in James that can be enhanced through deeper religious thought. Here we can begin to see the subtlety of Stowe's sketch emerge.

In courting George's favor as a means toward gaining the approval of his father, James finds himself gradually won over to a deepening religious commitment. When George dies before reaching his full potential as a minister-leader, James takes up the role, with Uncle Lot providing financial support for James's training. At the end of the story, as Grace and James are collaborating to provide spiritual leadership for Farmington, "one of [New England's] most thriving villages" (p. 23), we find that Stowe's sketch has a larger application beyond the single family level. James's successful courtship of Grace and her family has its more significant parallel in their courtship of him – winning the young man over to a social role beyond his own earlier self-expectations and, therefore, extending the power of places like little Newbury far beyond its seemingly contained village space. And, having demonstrated the impact of such apparently small-scale, family- and village-level experiences, Stowe and her story have carried out a courtship of their own – convincing the reader that places like the New England village have a key part to play in the larger welfare of the nation.

In the 1830s and 1840s, Stowe (along with Lydia Sigourney, Alice Cary and others) was one of the authors who helped establish the village sketch as a genre, and Stowe herself affiliated with a sub-genre using the form to envision New England as emblematic for the nation. Sandra Zagarell argues that, "At a time when non-Protestant immigrants were a source of distress to many native-born Americans and when the predominance of Anglo-Saxon New England seemed challenged by many changes, including . . . the diffusion of the nation beyond the Appalachians, a literature that conflated American community life with 'the' (generic) New England village" acted as a stabilizing force.[2]

On a second reading, therefore, Stowe's understated description of her setting on the story's opening pages carries more weight; her emphasis on the recurring patterns of life in Newbury conveys a broader social narrative, and we can hear a gentle irony in her friendly authorial voice:

> Did you ever see the little village of Newbury, in New England? I dare say you never did; for it was just one of those out-of-the-way places where nobody ever came unless they came on purpose: a green little hollow, wedged like a bird's nest between half a dozen high hills . . . The inhabitants were all of that respectable old standfast family who make it a point to be born, bred, married, to die, and be buried all in the selfsame spot . . . [A]s to manners, morals, arts, and sciences, the people

in Newbury always went to their parties at three o'clock in the afternoon, and came home before dark; always stopped all work the minute the sun was down on Saturday night; always went to meeting on Sunday; had a schoolhouse with all the ordinary inconveniences; were in neighborly charity with each other; read their Bibles, feared their God, and were content with such things as they had – the best philosophy after all." ("UL," pp. 4–5)

Re-reading this description after following the story to its conclusion, we can see that Stowe is offering her readers a map for nation-building, one individual (James Benton), one family (the Griswold–Benton union), one small town (Newbury and Farmington) at a time. Though she playfully suggests at the outset that New Englanders' relative contentment "with such things as they had" is the "best philosophy" they have to offer, her tracing of the complementary influence of George on James, and, ironically, of James on Uncle Lot, tracks a pattern of religion-based maturation extendable beyond these individuals. The possibility New England village life represents for the larger culture is, ultimately, embodied not just in its recurring social practices but also in its ability to reflect and grow to more advanced levels of thoughtful action – as seen in a sermon George preaches to his Newbury neighbors: "In the sermon, there was the strong intellectual nerve, the constant occurrence of argument and statement, which distinguishes a New England discourse; but it was touched with life by the intense, yet half-subdued, feeling with which he seemed to utter it. Like the rays of the sun, it enlightened and melted at the same moment" (p. 17).

In the sermon Stowe gives George to preach, as in the characterizations of Lot and Grace, the author signals what may be drawn from New England culture. She also anticipates what much of her future writing will offer to readers – a regionally based "sermon," with a "strong intellectual nerve" and a moral "argument," but also with "intense feeling."

Stowe's first readers for this story were fellow members of the Semicolon Club, the literary society to which she belonged while living in Ohio in the 1830s and 1840s. Their enthusiasm for the piece encouraged her to submit it to a contest, and her winning led to its publication in James Hall's Cincinnati magazine. When this and other sketches (originally published in periodicals ranging from Sarah Hale's *Lady's Book* to the *New York Evangelist*) were assembled into the *Mayflower* in 1842, the anthology met with only limited success. Re-issued in 1855 after the publication of *Uncle Tom's Cabin*, the book's sales predictably increased, though certainly never near the level of her major antislavery novel.

In "Uncle Lot" and the *Mayflower* collection as a whole, however, we can identify dimensions within Stowe's early writing that would carry over through her entire literary career. A major part of this profile would be to mine her New England heritage for appealing characters, recurring themes, and a representative setting to embody the values of her upbringing.

In Stowe's own introduction to the *Mayflower* collection, she credited both her membership in the Semicolon Club and her New England background as key sources for writing. On the one hand, Stowe reported that the *Mayflower* grew out of "the social literary parties of Cincinnati, for whose genial meetings many of these articles were prepared." On the other hand, her commentary explained, the collection also represented "a series of New England sketches," identifiable as much by a recurring subject (her home region) as by the occasion of their production (for sociable readers living in the west). In that second guise, Stowe said she named her sketches to associate them with "the descendants of the Puritans," whose New England home boasted the flower of the title – one living "in the edges of the woods about Plymouth," and thus "the first flower to salute the storm-beaten crew of the Mayflower," arriving from England.[3] Overall, then, by linking a desire to address her readers' needs (as represented by the Semicolon group) with material drawn from her own New England background, Stowe laid out a diagram that would guide her career. This agenda would produce writing grounded in one region and its values, but simultaneously extending beyond that source, based on an acute awareness of her audience.

By the time she wrote her *Mayflower* introduction, Stowe had already begun to explore strategies for reaching readers through a range of venues. Besides magazine pieces, she had published a well regarded geography textbook. These forays into the literary marketplace had been rather modest ones. Through much of the 1840s, although her husband encouraged her to write (for personal fulfillment, literary distinction, and additional family income), she had difficulty carving out time to do so, given the pressing duties of motherhood. But the turn into a new decade would bring national political issues to the foreground of her thinking, opening up a broader landscape for writing that would change her place in literary history forever. Even in that turning-point text of *Uncle Tom's Cabin*, however, as in the writing she would do through later decades, the imaginary New England community she had laid out in "Uncle Lot" would still play a crucial part.

Uncle Tom's Cabin

From its original publication in the *National Era*, an abolitionist periodical, Stowe's first novel-length narrative captured a far larger audience than could have been expected for an assault on slavery. Drawing many new readers to Gamaliel Bailey's weekly, the serial also laid the groundwork for the book version, which became an immediate and unprecedented bestseller, in the United States and abroad. For the rest of her life, Stowe would be known primarily for this text. Therefore, being the author of *Uncle Tom's Cabin's* would exert a powerful influence on her subsequent efforts to manage her professional identity.

Composing Uncle Tom's Cabin *for 1850s' periodical readers*

As Stowe's fame grew, she and other members of her family provided several different, somewhat contradictory stories about her composition process for her first and best-known anti-slavery narrative. That mythology helped promote a vision of her authorship as benevolently motivated, and even divinely guided – although her actual experiences of writing were (also) shaped by practical needs and strategies. Building Stowe's public image in her lifetime, the Beecher family's anecdotes about *Uncle Tom's Cabin* cast her writing process in feminized, moral terms. For example, one story portrayed Stowe as having an inspirational vision of Tom's death scene during a church service, then beginning her actual composing process by working backward from what would become the novel's climax. Associated with this tableau of Stowe's heavenly motivation to write were her own assertions that God was the true author of the text – a claim which reinforced the moral message of the narrative while also promoting Stowe as an unselfish Christian servant rather than a savvy manager of a worldly literary career.

Other accounts linked her writing of *Uncle Tom's Cabin* to an intense identification with slave mothers. Stowe regularly depicted herself as sharing the suffering of women whose children were sold away; she described achieving an empathetic connection with their pain when her own beloved child Charley died during a cholera epidemic in Cincinnati. Affiliating the moral message of the narrative with holy motherhood, this element in the novel's mythology appealed to a crucial core audience – white, middle-class mothers.

All the contemporary stories about Stowe's composing process do seem to agree on one crucial point – that the Fugitive Slave Law was a decisive spur to her writing. In the months after passage of the 1850 legislation, Stowe's favorite brother, Henry Ward Beecher, shifted his political position toward more active opposition to slavery. Up until then, he had organized such highly visible campaigns as fund-raising to buy the freedom of individual slaves during rousing services at his church in Brooklyn, while staking out a stance opposing both slavery and immediate abolition. That is, he felt, preserving the Union precluded sudden Emancipation in places where slavery already held sway, but preventing its spread into new areas was important. Now, in reaction to the 1850 law, Henry Ward Beecher argued against northerners' upholding the new legislative mandate that they directly aid in the return of fugitive slaves. In that vein, the charismatic preacher's March 1850 editorial in *The Independent* anticipated in expository form points Stowe would later take up through narrative in *Uncle Tom's Cabin*.

More directly and radically, another of Stowe's minister brothers, Edward Beecher, called her attention to individual cases in the north where the law was having its worst-case effects. On her way to set up housekeeping in Brunswick, Maine, where her husband Calvin was about to take up a new teaching position at Bowdoin College, Stowe stopped to visit in Boston. There Edward and his wife Isabella shared frightening tales not only of former slaves being forcibly returned to bondage but also of white Christian leaders being called upon to violate their personal principles by aiding such heinous deeds. In a letter sent to Stowe's son Charles years later as he was working on a biography of his mother, Mrs Edward Beecher recalled forwarding reports after Harriet had left Massachusetts for her new home in Maine:

> These terrible things which were going on in Boston were well calculated
> to rouse up this spirit. What can I do? I thought. Not much myself, but
> I know one who can. So I wrote several letters to your mother, telling
> her of various heart-rending events caused by the enforcement of
> the Fugitive Slave Law. I remember distinctly saying in one of them,
> "Now Hattie, if I could use a pen as you can, I would write something
> that would make this whole nation feel what an accursed thing slavery
> is."   (Qtd in Charles Stowe, *Life*, p. 145)

Charles Stowe's biography confirms this anecdote by offering a portrait of his mother's immediate resolve to carry out her sister-in-law's mandate, built on a shared understanding that to make readers "feel" the meaning of slavery – to engage with the issue emotionally – was the goal Harriet Beecher Stowe determined to address.

> Mrs. Stowe herself read [the letter] aloud to the assembled family, and
> when she came to the passage, "I would write something that would
> make the whole nation feel what an accursed thing slavery is," Mrs.
> Stowe rose up from her chair, crushing the letter in her hand, and with
> an expression on her face that stamped itself on the mind of her child,
> said: "I will write something. I will if I live."

Charles then depicts his mother as laboring over many succeeding months to write *Uncle Tom's Cabin* as a moral response to the Fugitive Slave Act. By December of 1850, her son explains, Stowe had begun to envision the serial, which she initially projected in a letter to her husband as simply "a sketch for the 'Era' on the capabilities of liberated blacks to take care of themselves" (Charles Stowe, *Life*, p. 147).

Bailey's *Era* was a hybrid publishing venue. The *Era* aimed at a mixed-gender, white, middle-class audience used to reading reports on national political issues alongside sentimental didactic stories and poetry.[4] Already well established enough to dwarf other anti-slavery periodicals, given its circulation of around 15,000 readers, the *Era* heightened its appeal by publishing such American literary figures as William Cullen Bryant, Sara Jane Clarke (writing as Grace Greenwood), and John Greenleaf Whittier. Editor Bailey himself described his periodical in these terms: "I have aimed to give it a two-fold character – that [of] a high-toned Literary paper, and that of a firm, consistent advocate of Human Rights."[5] More moderate than the *Liberator*, the *Era* avoided antagonizing southern readers, so much so that William Lloyd Garrison huffily demeaned its stance as "'milk and water' abolitionism."[6] But if the *Era* was less radical than the *Liberator*, it was also aligned with the tendency of many US periodicals then to assume the role literature should play as a social agent, not just an artistic object. Progressive in stance, the *Era* was relatively mainstream in both politics and aesthetics for an anti-slavery publication of its time – so ably positioned to help Stowe reach a large audience.

The periodical form did impose some constraints on Stowe's composing process, such as ever-looming deadlines and expectations for an episodic plot. Yet, like Charles Dickens, who had so successfully developed rhetorical strategies to maintain reader interest over the long reading time required for serials, Stowe also capitalized on the form through such tools as focus on a central character (in this case, Tom), creation of striking scenes, and building to compelling break points at the close of particular installments.[7] Breathless accounts of Dickens fans waiting at the pier for the newest copies of his stories to arrive in the US from England would now have counterparts in the enthusiastic letters fans wrote to the *Era*, responding to Stowe's evolving narrative. Thus, the serial form brought some important extra-textual benefits, such as the opportunity to draw encouragement from her audience, whose positive feedback Bailey sometimes reported directly in the periodical's pages. These letters could have been one factor leading the text to greater length than Stowe had originally intended, judging from occasions when Bailey shared reader sentiments that the author should stretch out her plot for continued reader enjoyment.

Had Gamaliel Bailey not provided such a congenial venue, would *Uncle Tom's Cabin* still have been written? Perhaps. But certainly not in the form that it assumed through its initial publication, in forty-one periodical install-ments over forty-four weeks. And, we should note, even the book version that appeared just as the serial was ending might not have been so astoundingly suc-cessful, without Bailey's publicity. Besides chronicling the novel's impressive sales in the US and abroad, for instance, Bailey defended *Uncle Tom's Cabin* from negative reviewers, and he even sold copies of the books in the offices of the *Era*.

Bailey's continued support of Stowe's work was probably not entirely unselfish. The serial version had helped push circulation of his weekly to a peak subscription level. Given that rise in circulation, Michael Winship's asser-tion that "Stowe surely earned the $400 that Bailey eventually paid her" for the narrative seems irrefutable.[8] And, understandably, he was hoping to retain her as a regular contributor. In many ways, the success of *Uncle Tom's Cabin* grew out of a fortunate match of theme and venue, author and editor.

According to Charles Stowe, the unfolding story of *Uncle Tom's Cabin* also grew from his mother's ongoing moves to identify imaginatively with slaves' lives, especially the break-up of families (which she continued to associate with her own loss of a child); the intense experiences of sharing and even crying over draft segments with her children; and her strategic efforts to gather relevant background information through such reliable sources as Frederick Douglass. Researching while she wrote, Stowe kept clearly in mind her belief that her white, middle-class audience would be best swayed through vivid pictures – concrete examples aimed at the heart. Thus, when contacting Douglass for details about life on a cotton plantation, she explained that she had already read "an able paper written by a Southern planter," but that she was "anxious to have something more from another standpoint," and that she hoped "to be able to make a picture that shall be graphic and true to nature in its details" (qtd in Charles Stowe, *Life*, p. 150). Even in reporting on his mother's research, Charles Stowe still insisted that her work came pouring out onto the page from "moral and religious exaltation," that it was a text "from the heart rather than the head," and that it represented "an outburst of deep feeling" rather than a product of professional craft. Harriet Beecher Stowe, he asserted, "had no more thought of style or literary excellence than the mother who rushes into the street and cries for help to save her children from a burning house" (p. 153).

While writing, Stowe capitalized on her Beecher family ties. For instance, she received important encouragement early on from her beloved brother Henry Ward Beecher, who visited Harriet's Maine home in early 1851, when the two siblings talked through a whole night about how they might both contribute to the battle against slavery. In that conversation, Thomas Gossett suggests, Henry probably had no conception of how his sister might eventually outstrip him as a famous campaigner for social justice, but the prominent Brooklyn pastor did affirm her writing plans and promise to solicit readers for her projected piece.[9] What seems to have been clear to both of them, even then, was the potential efficacy of supporting each other in this vital pastoral work.

In a version of what Ann Douglas has described as the ongoing alliance between male ministers and the women who were the most active participants in American religious life, Stowe was assuming a literary version of the preacher role that her brothers and father had always claimed. And her family full of ministers was providing a strong sustaining force. Douglas argued in her groundbreaking book that "the nineteenth-century minister moved in a world of women," preaching "mainly to women" and "work[ing] not only for them but with them, in mission and charity work of all kinds." Thus, "Female 'influence,' whether he liked it or not, was the minister's chief support; maternal power was a model of action with complex relevance to his own performance because it was his prime channel of communication."[10] In the context of Douglas's argument, Stowe's moving into an activist, preacher-like brand of anti-slavery writing was consistent not only with her family's involvement in the ministry, but with her circle's view of middle-class women as closely allied with Christian social intervention – to the extent that religion and clergy were both, in fact, dependent on "female 'influence'" as an active social force. So, as she began Uncle Tom's Cabin, Stowe would have seen the work she was doing in religious terms, as she had her earlier pro-temperance writing, with the text itself envisioned as joining Protestant culture's continued effort to shape the American nation.

Overall, highlighting the multifaceted, contradictory features in accounts of its composition is an important step toward recognizing the complexity of Uncle Tom's Cabin. In the myths Stowe's family circulated to build the novel's history, after all, we see a striking blend of moral commitment and practical considerations, religious fervor and calculated management of the writing task at hand, tearful feelings and purposeful research, dedication to a radical cause and hope for steady income. Given that this complicated array of influences operated throughout the many months of Stowe's writing, it is hardly surprising that her novel wound up assembling such disparate elements in its plot, characters, and themes.

Black masculinity in Uncle Tom's Cabin

Reading Uncle Tom's Cabin today will likely be a surprising experience for anyone who has come to know Stowe and her title character based on their recurring depictions in popular culture, rather than through a direct encounter with her text itself. Indeed, a careful study of the novel today entails peeling back layer upon layer of versions of "Uncle Tom" and *Uncle Tom's Cabin* from our cultural memory, so that we can engage the narrative on its own terms as a starting point for more critical understanding. That process requires recognizing the highly rhetorical nature of the story that Stowe crafted with a very particular audience in mind. Then we can retrace the extended culture-making processes that have refashioned the author and her characters to fit the needs of many later audiences. After all, generations of later readers have come to this capacious, flexible, and generative text for many different purposes than those who first turned the pages of the *National Era* in the 1850s. And, even in Stowe's own time, the text was controversial, eliciting a wide range of responses linked to intense literary politics, as well as race, gender, regional, and social class issues. (See Chapter 4.)

We begin our peeling-back process with the core plot as organized around its major black male characters: Tom and George Harris. Despite the title's emphasis on one character, *Uncle Tom's Cabin* actually presents two contrasting narratives of heroic attempts to escape slavery's dehumanization. As the narrative opens, in the border state of Kentucky, both Tom and George find their families jeopardized by one of the evils that Stowe is most set on attacking – sales that separate families. Tom's master Mr Shelby is about to sell two slaves to redress a slipping financial situation. The "things" selected for sale are actually among the family's favorites: Tom, known for his Christian devotion and hard work; and young Harry, the winsome child of Mrs Shelby's maid Eliza and George Harris (who is owned by a different master). Whereas Tom acquiesces to the sale out of loyalty, Eliza resolves to flee with her child to save Harry from the dreaded slave trader, Haley.

One narrative trajectory follows Tom's experiences as he is sold further and further south, winding up on the plantation of the archetypically cruel Simon Legree before earning Christian salvation through suffering. A second plotline moves northward rather than southward, tracking the family of George Harris from initial separation through reunion. At the end of the novel, the Harris family has emigrated to Africa. Tom's noble suffering and death have inspired young George Shelby (son of Tom's original master) to free all the family slaves and to plan for their future education.

Stowe designs her account of Tom's being sold away from his home and never returning to elicit sentimental sympathy from her readers – an emotional identification process that will help her audience to see slaves as fully human and, therefore, to oppose slavery. Driving him from Kentucky to the darkest of Louisiana swamps, slavery takes Tom further and further away from his earthly family – his wife Aunt Chloe and their small sons – before finally granting him entry into the utopian family of holy martyrdom.

At various points, Tom is heroic in the traditional, worldly sense. For example, soon after meeting Evangeline (Eva) St Clare and her father, he boldly rescues the child from drowning when she falls from a steamboat into the river. Stowe's casting of Tom as "broad-chested" and "strong-armed" as "he caught her in his arms" is telling at this point.[11] Such details emphasize his strength and courage, belying the stereotype of a weak old man that has grown up through re-configurations of his character over time. Later, at Legree's plantation, comparing the slave Cassy's situation to that of Daniel in the lion's den, Tom persuades her to escape, then steadfastly refuses to give up information that would allow her villainous master to recapture her and her young companion Emmeline (p. 563). He endures brutal torture from Legree and that reprobate's two most corrupted slaves, Sambo and Quimbo, rather than endanger the escapees.

Though Tom's refusal to fight back against Legree at this stage may seem unmanly, even unrealistic, Stowe clearly intended for her original readers to view this choice in idealized terms associated with Christian service. She dubs him a "martyr," and even has his unwavering faith motivate Quimbo and Sambo to beg Tom's forgiveness and embrace Christ themselves. For Stowe, Tom's request to the Lord to "give me these two more souls, I pray" would have reemphasized to her readers that his decision to remain behind when Cassy and Emmeline fled was itself a mark of heroism (p. 585). When Cassy had begged "Father Tom" to join her flight and embrace personal freedom, he refused on grounds linked to a spiritual strength in the face of Legree's worldly brute authority: "time was when I would [have fled]; but the Lord's given me a work among these yer poor souls, and I'll stay with 'em and bear my cross with 'em till the end" (562). Embracing a Christ-like death, Tom represents a sacrificial brand of heroism that would have had great appeal to Stowe's original audience.

Given that Stowe was writing primarily for the *white* middle-class readers whom she perceived as most able to exercise political power over the slavery issue, we should position *Uncle Tom's Cabin* in that initial rhetorical context. Then we can see ways in which Tom's character was designed to draw potentially resistant whites to her view of slavery's evils and blacks' worthiness. Particularly important is the fact that, in the 1850s, fears associated with slave insurrections fed anxieties about black men's supposed propensity to aggression; also, many white middle-class Americans still viewed blacks as inherently less than human. In such a context, Stowe's strategy for characterizing Tom's brand of heroism, and especially her approach for making his spiritual leadership unthreatening to whites, becomes understandable.

However frustrating Tom's passivity may be to us today, Stowe's first readers would have recognized (and appreciated) links between his model of heroism and an ideal of spiritualized masculinity being touted by abolitionist movement leaders. They sought to replace what had been the dominant ideal of American manliness – aggressively power-seeking – with an emphasis on true manhood as imitating the model of Jesus, who combined strength with loving generosity, thereby replacing competitiveness with techniques of moral suasion. This model, closely tied to a "doctrine of fraternal love," certainly had its opponents, among them prominent black men in the abolitionist movement, but it was also influential.[12]

Stowe's own family background is also important to consider in this regard. The daughter, sister, and wife of ministers, she had numerous personal models of male social activism closely tied to emulating Jesus. While readers coming to the novel today are often troubled by Stowe's choice to have Tom embody patient suffering and eventual martyrdom, her own male role models would have viewed Tom's character as exemplary. Like her brother Henry Ward Beecher, who was then using his pulpit to highlight the evils of slavery by depicting the Christ-like suffering of individual slaves, and who would later choose a book-length celebration of Jesus as a career-culminating project, Stowe knew the powerful appeal that the figure of Jesus held in the lives of her core audience. Lyman Abbott's 1903 authorial preface to a biography of Henry Ward Beecher himself is worth noting as an example. Looking back over a long personal relationship with the charismatic New York minister, Abbott used words applicable to Stowe's Tom to explain why Beecher's ministry had been so influential: "I obtained through him a new experience of God, of Christ, of salvation, of religion: I began to see that Jesus Christ was what God eternally is, ... [and] that religion is not the obedience of a reluctant soul to law, but the glad captivity of a loyal soul to the best of all loved friends" (Abbott, *Henry Ward Beecher*, p. xxix).

Still, however much she longed to advance a manhood tied to Christian virtue, Stowe seems to have realized that presenting Tom as the sole representative of black manliness would be insufficient to her argument against slavery. Thus, in contrast to Tom's patient suffering, she has George Harris enact a more activist brand of race-based leadership, seizing the right to individual freedom. Tom's version of Christian manhood resists one set of stereotypes southerners had been using to justify slavery – the recurring image of black men as savages needing the firm hand of the patriarchal institution to keep them under control. (Parallel characterizations of Native Americans were invoked in the Jacksonian period, we should note, to argue for Indian Removal, and would continue to be deployed to rationalize later efforts to manage the United States' Indian "problem," including white-run schools that aimed to "civilize.") But another element in whites' recurring representations of blacks was an ideology stressing their purportedly child-like natures.[13] With his repeated assertions of individual rights and his bold actions to claim them, George resists the stereotype that argued for slavery's necessity on the grounds that blacks were unable to care of themselves. Decisive, capable, and even daring, George is heroic in a more worldly sense than Tom, whose leadership is of a spiritual nature. (Stowe's description to her husband of how she planned to demonstrate "the capabilities of liberated blacks to take care of themselves" is interesting to revisit in this context, especially given her choice to make Tom, rather than George, the title character.)

When we first meet George, before he is even aware that Mr Shelby may be selling Harry, we already see a far more assertive figure than Tom. George is owned by a different master, a small-minded man who grants few privileges and is threatening new abuses. George has become so frustrated at slavery's injustices that he is preparing for flight to Canada, where he hopes to raise enough money to buy the freedom of his wife and child. Though Eliza is at first frightened by George's bold talk, this dream of freedom in the north may actually be the source of her desperate plan to carry Harry away from the Shelbys', once she finds out that her master has promised her son to the obnoxious Haley. Through a series of dramatic episodes including wild chases, disguises, and romantic reunions, the plotline for George and his family plays out with all the intensity of today's action movies, and with George exhibiting heroic traits consistent with that framework. The interwoven sequence of episodes centered on George Harris serves as a strong counterpoint to those depicting Tom's passivity in the face of slavery's cruelty.

There are some problems, though, with this argument. For one thing, Tom claims much more time (i.e., more pages) in the narrative than does George Harris. For another, whereas Tom is cast as a "pure" black, George is a mulatto; hence, the two characters are not set up as neat opposites for two different approaches of blacks' responding to slavery, since Stowe often suggests that George's more forceful traits are directly related to his white blood. Accordingly, readers should note that George's worldly victory over slavery may be, in Stowe's view, more attributable to assertive character traits "naturally" associated with his white blood rather than with an effort on her part to present a balanced portrayal of two black heroes choosing different courses of action through equally framed agency and ability.

Controversies over Stowe's ending

If we consider the text's repeated gestures toward presenting itself as an examination of American national values, then Stowe's positioning of *both* black male leaders outside the avenues to political power at the end of the novel is certainly important. The end points of Tom's and George's contrasting stories do combine to signal Stowe's highly conflicted position toward blacks' place in American culture during her own day, versus her seeming confidence in enlightened white males' capacity for political leadership. She has another George – young George Shelby, son of Tom's original master – rush to save Tom from Legree and, though failing in that attempt, free all the family's slaves and promise to educate them. She may mean to suggest that having George Shelby take on the role of "Liberator" in the next-to-last chapter mitigates the death of Tom as an individual, and even renders it more powerful in the long run. George Shelby's action does hold out the hope of freedom for a whole society of slaves now living in the south, a society represented synecdochically by the now-reformed Shelby plantation. And, Stowe might point out, Tom is the one whose death has inspired young master Shelby to swear that "from this hour, I will do what one man can to drive out this curse of slavery from my land!" (*UTC*, p. 593).

But what are we to make of Stowe's having this same George Shelby strike the unrepentant Legree an "indignant blow," which "knocked Legree flat upon his face"? This bold, avenging "Kentucky boy" then stands "over [Legree], blazing with wrath and defiance," a forceful white hero giving "no bad personification of his great namesake triumphing over the dragon" (p. 592). Why is it righteously saint-like for George Shelby to strike Legree down, though for Tom only *feminized* patience had been the proper choice? Why is the white man praised for enacting a brand of religious leadership (equated with dragon-killing) incorporating earthly power, whereas Tom's Christianity must be contained in suffering? However conscious we should be of Stowe's wish to appeal to her original white audience, we must also consider that her own personal assumptions about race-based limitations – ideas which we would certainly consider racist today – may also be at work in this characterization. Indeed, even George Shelby's description of the post-manumission relationship to be cultivated with his freed slaves underscores a persistent sense of superiority, with its references to white administration of the plantation needing to continue, along with his projected management of former slaves' learning.

The end point of George Harris's adventures is also significant. After seeming to grant the Harris family full-fledged freedom via their dramatic escape-to-Canada story, Stowe redirects their positive south-to-north plot trajectory by sending the entire family "back" to Africa, thereby affiliating with the Liberia colonization agenda already being decried by influential African American leaders in her own day.

When she wrote *Uncle Tom's Cabin*, Stowe was well aware of the on-going controversy over the colonization movement. The American Coloniza-tion Society (ACS), a group supporting the "return" of US-based slaves to an African "homeland," had been founded in 1816 by Robert Finley, and had racist ideas about the limitations of blacks. Leaders like Finley openly admitted that one goal of the society was to rid America of former slaves through a plan that would also uplift Africa, since Christianized blacks could Americanize and thus reform Liberia. Another goal aligned with many white leaders' racist perspec-tives involved preventing long-term miscegenation within the United States, which leaders no less revered than Thomas Jefferson (ironically, given his own mixed-race children!) consistently cast as a dangerous problem to be avoided. ACS membership rolls boasted such white leaders as Speaker of the House Henry Clay and General (later President) Andrew Jackson. Opponents such as John Quincy Adams resisted the plans for an American colony of former slaves as unconstitutional. Many free black leaders in the north were also opposed, arguing that a growing number of African Americans had been brought up in the United States. As leaders such as James Forten noted: "Whereas our ances-tors (not of choice) were the first successful cultivators of the wilds of America, we their descendants feel ourselves entitled to participate in the blessings of her luxuriant soil, which their blood and sweat manured."[14] Meanwhile, in Liberia itself, efforts to establish the colony were met by resistance from local tribes, who often viewed the blacks seeking to settle there as interlopers.

By the time Stowe wrote her first anti-slavery novel, the ACS had been under attack, both in Africa and in the US, for a long time. However, a number of black American leaders did welcome the opportunity to settle in Liberia, seeing it as an escape not only from slavery but also from white racism in the US northern cities. And some influential white Americans – including Stowe's father Lyman Beecher – continued to support the ACS. Stowe's personal position on the colonization question may, in fact, have been shaped by Lyman Beecher's difficult experience trying to deal with a vocal group of students at Lane Seminary, so opposed to the movement that they led a protest at the school and eventually dropped out, choosing to enroll at Oberlin instead. Always inclined to support her family members in such trying times, Stowe and her husband Calvin repeatedly affirmed their backing of Beecher, even up to the time when he gave up the struggle to keep Lane Seminary open, by retiring in the same year that *Uncle Tom's Cabin* began appearing in the *National Era*. Stowe was, nonetheless, also an attentive reader of audience responses to her writing. So later, when a number of leading blacks criticized her novel's depiction of the Harrises and others as emigrating to Liberia, she responded by asserting (whether shrewdly or sincerely) that she had never been a strong supporter of colonization herself. In fact, Stowe's personal stance on the issue was complex and evolving. She had written Frederick Douglass a letter in July of 1851 urging him to modify his own anti-colonization views. But she made multiple moves, over time, to distance herself from the ACS and its overtly racist attitudes, especially its association with a wish to purge America of blacks. By 1853, she was going so far as to say that, were she to be writing *Uncle Tom's Cabin* at that point, she would not be including the Liberia migration in her plot.[15]

However her stance may have changed over time, Stowe's first anti-slavery novel certainly undercuts its own affirmation of black civic leadership in George Harris by evacuating his family from the American national landscape. She has Harris tout the African colony for providing "a tangible, separate existence" for American blacks (*UTC*, p. 608). With its chilling anticipation of the *separate but equal* doctrine that would dominate the American legal system on into the twentieth century, George Harris's declaration is grounded in two contradictory impulses – an assertion of blacks' capability to lead a republic, on the one hand, and a refusal to conceive of their doing so within the United States, on the other. Stowe does have George Harris "grant that this Liberia may have subserved all sorts of purposes, by being played off, in the hands of our oppressors, against us" (*UTC*, p. 609). But she still insists that this African nation, modeled on the American system, is the best answer available to ambitious and capable black men like George.

Stowe's choice for the Harrises to emigrate may represent a logical extension of the author's emphasis on blacks' capabilities and on the related aim of undermining southern arguments that slavery, based on a family model, was justified by blacks' inescapable dependency. Pointing out that both Topsy and George willingly claim the role of benevolent Christian leadership in Africa, Susan Ryan argues that Stowe may have intended this choice to underscore black independence from even the most charitable forms of white control: "By choosing Africa as the site of their good works, Topsy and the Harris family . . . . defy the pro-slavery faction's claim that slaves . . . could never attain basic economic security, much less benevolent agency, on their own. Moreover, the former slaves' move to Liberia also allows them to distance themselves . . . from ties of gratitude and obligation . . . that benevolent rhetoric insisted should structure their relationships with their Northern benefactors."[16]

While Ryan's insights certainly resonate with Stowe's initial plan to write about liberated blacks' capabilities, the novel's own dependence on the rhetoric of religious benevolence and nationhood as primarily a white prerogative may ultimately undercut this aim. Let us note George Harris's own language for justifying blacks' "return" to Africa:

> In these days, a nation is born in a day. A nation starts, now, with all the great problems of republican life and civilization wrought out to its hand; – it has not to discover, only to apply. Let us, then, all take hold together, with all our might, and see what we can do with this new enterprise, and the whole splendid continent of Africa opens before us and our children. Our nation shall roll the tide of civilization and Christianity along its shores, and plant there mighty republics, that, growing with the rapidity of tropical vegetation, shall be for all coming ages.   (*UTC*, p. 609)

Stowe's metaphor-mixing is striking here. On the one hand, the Liberian nation will be easy to develop, because blacks need only "to apply" the lessons already learned through the model of republican government provided by white leadership in America. (Blacks, ever the students of superior whites, do not "discover" truths themselves but instead translate white knowledge and skills into a new context.) On the other hand, this process is depicted as naturally occurring in the welcoming climate of an Africa where republican values, having been "plant[ed] there," will be "growing with the rapidity of tropical vegetables." Stowe uses yet another implicit metaphor to bridge the seeming contradiction between these two images of whites modeling republican government for blacks and African republics sprouting naturally, in profusion, in a "tropical" setting. The mediating force, according to George Harris (and Stowe), has been and will continue to be Christianity, source of "civilization" for blacks. Even in migration, George Harris and his "separate" people will be guided by the influence of Protestant Christianity, as embodied in figures like George Shelby.

Racial essentialism in Uncle Tom's Cabin

One factor behind the limitations Stowe sets for her black characters in *Uncle Tom's Cabin* was the racial essentialism so prevalent during her time. Like many other whites who opposed slavery, and despite her progressive view of slaves as human beings rather than chattel, Stowe did not perceive blacks as having the same capabilities as the "Anglo-Saxon" race with which she self-identified and which she has George Harris designate as having been "intrusted" to establish "the destinies of the world" (*UTC*, p. 610). In that context, Arthur Riss calls on us to recognize that "the assumption that race crucially formed personal and national identity thoroughly pervaded antebellum culture" and that Stowe's own "particular version of racial essentialism . . . advocates the abolition of slavery not by discrediting racialism but by advocating a stronger sense of biological racialism."[17] Along those lines, Stowe associated the strong character traits she did give to George and Eliza with their mixed-race status – specifically with their white blood.

Meanwhile, she cast a number of traits associated with idealized Christianity as "naturally" accessible to blacks through the essential, biology-based traits of their racial identities. For instance, she repeatedly praised Tom for his stoicism, generosity, and dedication, connecting such traits with his becoming a spiritual hero. She made clear that these positive characteristics were affirmed by whites such as Eva St Clare and George Shelby, who guide Tom's literacy acquisition, his related Bible study, and thus his moral development. At the same time, though, she repeatedly associated Tom's religious behavior (and that of other admirable black characters) with blacks' "natural" affinity for the elements of Christianity that promote child-like affection, docility, and emotion.

Stowe's anti-slavery argument benefited from this stance by inviting white readers to recognize elements of humanity in blacks that were strategically linked to a parallel belief about gender and identity. After all, the ways in which women were "naturally" more inclined to be affectionate, docile, and emotional – and thus well suited to be moral guides for their families – resonated with the tendencies supposedly inherent in "the African race." However, her racial essentialism also had a number of negative implications for her novel's black characters in the long run, similar to the ways in which ideologies of gender identity have continued, over time, to constrain women's place in American culture. Thus, Stowe assigned Tom a number of quite demeaning traits that she linked to the (supposedly) inherent aspects of his racial identity – his essential blackness.

For instance, when he arrives at the St Clares' home in New Orleans, Stowe renders Tom's pleasure at his new surroundings in terms that emphasize the distance between his unrefined pleasure in the scene and his master's more studied attitude. Declares Stowe: "The negro ... is an exotic ..., and he has, deep in his heart, a passion for all that is splendid, rich, and fanciful; a passion which, rudely indulged by an untrained taste, draws on them [i.e., blacks] the ridicule of the colder and more correct white race" (*UTC*, p. 253). Along those lines, Stowe's depictions of Tom sometimes echo a tendency among whites of her day to vacillate between attributing exotically alluring features to blacks and seeking to contain those very traits with complex rhetorical counter-moves, which in *Uncle Tom's Cabin* generally emphasize the purportedly essential humility of negroes as drawing them to Christianity and away from the kind of earthly "passion" invoked in the description of her hero above.

In addition to the stereotypes of feminized Christianity associated with Tom, Stowe played on equally troubling (if more simplified) caricatures for other black male characters in the novel by drawing on the minstrel tradition that was well established in 1850s American culture. By the time Stowe wrote *Uncle Tom's Cabin*, minstrelsy's complex forms had worked their way into even the most proper of middle-class homes, via such avenues as parlor plays and sheet music for minstrel-tradition songs like those of Stephen Foster (who had been a resident of Cincinnati, when the Beecher family lived there). Therefore, Stowe had ready access to minstrelsy's stereotypes. Like other women of her social class, she would not have attended the performances. Until melodramas like those based on *Uncle Tom's Cabin* emerged later in the century, minstrel shows targeted working-class male audiences such as Irish immigrants, whose own precarious social status helped shape the genre. In Linda Williams's view, in fact, the spectators typically attending antebellum blackface comedy performances were drawn to the form through both identifying and distancing impulses (i.e., sharing a resistance against white Protestant behavioral norms, like that of the comic figures depicted in blackface shows, but also using those same routines to cultivate a sense of superiority).[18]

This ambivalence on the part of white audiences toward the figures in minstrel shows, meanwhile, reflected and encouraged more widespread attitudes in the larger culture, thereby reinforcing the appeal of the form. It was the most popular entertainment in the US at the time when Stowe was creating *Uncle Tom's Cabin*. And part of minstrelsy's appeal lay in its ability to blend multiple perspectives on race into a single performance. A show might shift from a song portraying slavery as easy fun, in line with blacks' "inherently" limited capacities, to a subversive critique embedded in a scene depicting clever resistance. Given this double-edged context, Stowe's use of various features from blackface minstrelsy in her novel is not only understandable; it is practically predictable.

In Stowe's rendering, blackface-based comedy plays a complex role consistent with Eric Lott's argument that antebellum minstrelsy negotiated a contradictory terrain incorporating both racist (and therefore highly constraining) delineations of black character and "a celebration of an authentic people's culture, the dissemination of black arts with potentially liberating results."[19] In one sequence, for example, the farcical Sam and Andy undercut sympathy-oriented portrayals of characters like Tom. In the midst of melodrama inviting the audience to identify with the plight of George Harris, Harry and Eliza, Stowe suddenly presents Sam and Andy as shuffling, laughable stereotypes, so that our empathy for the escaping slaves is at least temporarily disrupted by comedy's distancing effect. Encountering such caricatures is certainly troubling for today's readers. Stowe's first audience was probably far from disturbed, however, since the minstrel show conventions the author incorporated for Sam and Andy, as well as for characters such as Topsy and Harry Harris (both labeled

"Jim Crow" figures by Stowe) were permeating the culture, both in the US and in Europe.

By the 1840s and 1850s, minstrelsy was evolving from a form targeted primarily at working-class male audiences to new iterations, with some abolitionist performers like the Hutchinson family singers even attempting to tap into its conventions, adapting its entertaining elements to promote serious causes. Hence, Stowe's initial readers may well have been able to recognize both humor and progressive claims of blacks' capability in scenes like the one where Mrs Shelby purportedly urges Sam and Andy to aid Haley's pursuit of Eliza while cleverly signaling that she really has very different intentions for them to address. A close reading of the exchanges between Mrs Shelby and the two slaves, and between the same two men and Haley, does indicate that the most shambling-seeming machinations tap into such minstrel show conventions as the black end man's responses to an interlocutor's corrective directions (here enacted by Mrs Shelby, Sarah Meer finds). These comic language games may be played to purposeful effect. Such a reading can help account for the remarkable success *Uncle Tom's Cabin* had in reaching far broader audiences than earlier anti-slavery works had been able to do. That is, says Meer, Stowe's "nods to minstrelsy . . . did more than provide comic relief; by turning the end man–interlocutor dialogues into conduits for disguised and ambivalent sympathy for slave characters, they may have made its anti-slavery message palatable for the cautious and scarcely noticeable for the indifferent."[20] Perhaps, then, the racist attitudes firmly entrenched in her minstrelsy-based characterizations were as untroubling to Stowe as they would have been to the many Americans who did attend the shows – or who, gathered around a middle-class parlor piano, sang racist lyrics drawn from that tradition. In any case, we should note her inclusion of such tried-and-true minstrelsy features as Topsy's malapropisms and Harry Harris's imitations of a deformed old man, hobbling and spitting (*UTC*, pp. 355–64; 44).

Even more importantly, we should question the sources and the implications of our own responses to these episodes. Indeed, part of what may make today's readers uncomfortable with such scenes is our tacit realization that Stowe's original audience – and, by implication, Stowe herself – could so easily accommodate both the denigrating aspects of the two black men's characterizations and the trickster-like skill beneath their masks. In those equally available readings, we may well recognize our own capacity for identifying the target of satire in a stand-up comic's routine or a television show's skit while still laughing (not guiltily enough?) at the more offensive elements in the joke. Sam's ironic scolding of Andy for impeding Haley's efforts to catch Eliza, along with their joint conniving to send Haley in a direction different than that actually taken by the slave mother and her child, does signal one of the strategies slaves used for resistance in the face of power, but it also assumes that readers will find real humor in the minstrel show echoes within these exchanges (*UTC*, pp. 113–20). So, by presenting *both* a trickster *and* a buffoon "take" on the black men simultaneously, Stowe enables divergent readings of the characters.

To delve a bit deeper into the nineteenth-century appeal and the enduring social implications of her choices here, we might consider reading Stowe's portrayal of Sam and Andy comparatively. In some ways, for instance, her treatment of these two figures anticipates (and perhaps even facilitates) later black male characters in American literature, ranging from Mark Twain's Jim in *The Adventures of Huckleberry Finn* to Charles Chesnutt's Uncle Julius in *The Conjure Woman* stories.

On the one hand, the odd blend of "fun" and discomfort we find in encountering Sam and Andy's "antics" presages many readerly reactions to Huck's jokes on Jim during their journey down the Mississippi, as Twain would craft it later in the century. In particular, we can see parallels between the use of dialect as a source of entertainment and the sometimes bumbling efforts of the black male figures to handle their interactions with whites through minstrelsy-oriented behaviors. If Twain appears to give Jim far more dignity for much of the late-century novel, that respectful treatment is at least partially un-done in the disquieting sequence near the end of that narrative when Huck holds Jim captive – literally re-enslaves the man who had been a loyal companion – in a shed, with ongoing encouragement from Tom Sawyer. Accordingly, although Jim may not have become the focal point of African American readers' objections to the extent that Uncle Tom has been, his depiction has certainly raised questions about Twain's text, including its suitability for classroom instruction in today's multiracial schools. For both Stowe and her longtime Hartford neighbor Samuel Clemens (Twain), it seems, being a defender and supporter of American blacks did not preclude the authors' tapping into racist attitudes to broaden their writings' appeal. In that regard, we might take note of the ways in which both of these anti-slavery narratives – *Uncle Tom's Cabin* and *The Adventures of Huckleberry Finn* – inspired quite a number of racist illustrations in book editions over the years, continually tapping into and reinforcing minstrelsy's well-known caricatures.

In contrast, when the African American author Charles Chesnutt created his humorous Uncle Julius character for the conjure stories he originally sold to *Atlantic Monthly* at the turn into the twentieth century, he too drew on stereotypes associated with mass culture's representations of southern black slave men, but to a very different effect. Imagining a freed slave still living, a squatter of sorts, in his former plantation home, Chesnutt shows Julius using cleverly wrought stories of slavery days to exercise control over the homeplace's new owner, a northerner (John) who has moved south with a sensitive wife (Annie). Like Stowe in her treatment of Sam and Andy collaborating with Mrs Shelby, Chesnutt positions Julius as forging an alliance with Annie, whose "readings" of Julius's stories are far more enlightened than her husband's. There is a clear difference, however, in the nature of the comic resonance at work in *Uncle Tom's Cabin* and that in Chesnutt's stories, adept though both may be at invoking cultural stereotypes. Chesnutt's Julius tells his own stories and through them claims a more assertive brand of cultural capital. In contrast, Stowe's Sam/Andy model for comic story-telling is led by the white-orchestrated performance of Mrs Shelby and remains completely inaccessible to Haley, who cannot even conceive of blacks' capacity to manipulate a situation. This distance between the white woman writer Stowe's ambivalent moves to appropriate minstrelsy and the black author Chesnutt's crafty assertion of a trickster humor marks the space between her romantic racialism (however "sympathetic") and his far more forceful reconfiguration of the dominant culture's stereotypes via a folk culture model linked to race-based riffing.[21] In this distance, we should recognize the racist elements in Stowe's text – making her both a product and a shaper of her day's culture.

If Stowe's treatment of characters like Sam and Andy (and later, Topsy) is sometimes difficult to decode, there can be little doubt where she stands on a figure like Augustine St Clare's slave Adolph. The spoiled and effeminate valet (with his "scented hair," his "opera glass" and the "elegant figured satin vest" he is always "sporting") invokes the ridiculous black dandy figure of stage shows and advertising cards, Zip Coon. Whether equating Adolph with a "puppy" or having young Harry Harris entertain the slaver Haley and Mr Shelby, as the child does "one of those wild, grotesque songs common among the negroes," Stowe repeatedly cast her minor black male characters as performers reinforcing white fantasies of essentialist racial identity (pp. 256; 44). In such scenes, she tapped into and also reinforced "Sambo" stereotypes that positioned blacks as child-like entertainers for whites, caricatures that were simultaneously serving "to subordinate" blacks on into the twentieth century.[22]

Stowe's treatment of black minor characters also ratifies a need for whites to control African Americans. Upon first arriving home to New Orleans with Eva and Tom, for instance, St Clare is faced with such an enthusiastic rushing forward by his slaves, who are wildly happy to see him, that he almost "stumbled over a sooty little urchin, who was crawling upon all fours," and thus had to warn his charges to "take yourselves off, like good boys and girls," whose frantic behavior needs to be tamed by the bag of treats ("apples, nuts, candy, ribbons, laces, and toys") that Eva has brought as gifts (*UTC*, p. 256).

In more ominous terms, Sambo and Quimbo, who have taken on the role of abusing fellow slaves on Legree's plantation, embody the stereotyped brute that was already associated with whites' fear of black insurrection. So, they forecast a type to be reinscribed in subsequent decades, in texts such as the film *Birth of a Nation*, to justify post-Civil War oppression of African Americans by groups like the Ku Klux Klan. Significantly, though these two fearsome characters are eventually redeemed by Tom, this reclamation is achieved only through Protestant – read white-managed – American cultural power.

Uncle Tom's Cabin *as gendered moral suasion*

As suggested by the above image of Eva dispensing gifts, Stowe attempted to navigate potentially troubling scenarios of cross-race relations by positioning *white females* as discreet managers of American society, charged not only with "taming" blacks but also with raising white children and guiding white men. In that context, we do well to remember that Stowe's original publication venue of the *Era* and her own practice of authorship up to this time supposed mixed-gender audiences reading literature together within American homes – with motherly teacher figures as the key interpreters of such texts' implications for the nation's welfare. In her own at-home teaching of her children, in her pre-authorial career as a seminary instructor, in the mother-celebrating educational writings of her older sister Catharine, and in the literary texts she read and produced in the decades before *Uncle Tom's Cabin*, Stowe repeatedly affirmed a vision of American maternal figures claiming public influence through their domestic direction of moral family literacy.

It is this insistent focus on female didactic energy that drives much of the action in *Uncle Tom's Cabin*, in spite of its title's designation of a male central character. Among many of the novel's first readers and more recent feminist scholars, the narrative's endorsement of motherly influence over American society and its worries over slavery's corruption of the domestic sphere have served as the basis for enthusiastic responses to the text. Two episodes were particularly popular with readers in Stowe's own day: the death of Eva St Clare and the escape of Eliza and Harry to freedom, aided by a white senator's wife. Both scenes tapped into conventions associated with sentimental literature and Protestant religious culture to support Stowe's overarching arguments. Both endorse feminine moral suasion as a prime force for effecting social change. In specific terms, Stowe's novel tapped into a theory very appealing to white middle-class women of her day: the idea that they could best shape the future of the nation by modeling moral principles in the home.

The death of little Eva became the centerpiece of many later cultural products spun off from *Uncle Tom's Cabin*, including art works as well as highly dramatic stagings. Jane Tompkins observed in her pivotal defense of Stowe's novel that this episode became the one "most often cited [derisively] as the epitome of Victorian sentimentalism . . . because it [was] the kind of incident most offensive to the sensibilities of twentieth-century academic critics."[23] Yet, as Tompkins and other feminist explicators of *Uncle Tom's Cabin*'s cultural work have pointed out, stories like little Eva's death carried enormous sentimental power for Stowe's original audience in the very traits that made them unappealing for readers of later eras. Children often died young in nineteenth-century America, and spiritually inflected deaths like Eva St Clare's were both a realistic occurrence in middle-class homes and a social practice families admired in a self-consciously religious culture. Pointedly allied with visions of Christian sacrifice, Eva's death prepared antebellum readers to accept Tom's choice of Christ-like martyrdom later in the novel. Eva's becoming a child-like angel argued in tear-inducing terms for readers to embrace a higher moral law and a purer vision of American society than that represented by slavery.

Reading not just about Eva's death itself but also about its eventual reformative effect on others like her father and Topsy, Stowe's audience would have understood the didactic message embedded in the mourning characters' tears – that embracing Eva's vision of Christ could save America. Otherwise, Eva's pious death showed, the sin of slavery would continue claiming not just black victims, but white children like the angelic child herself and, by extension, the American nation's future. With a compelling appeal to emotion, Eva's death spoke to readers in a feminized language of feeling consistent with the ideology of moral suasion, which was also at the heart of pedagogical practices and didactic texts well regarded by many middle-class women *and* men in Stowe's own time. Offering a vision of feminized saintliness, Eva affiliated with such ideological models as the "angel of the house," a trope emphasizing the efficacy of female moral influence, here exercised over both blacks and whites. Meanwhile, in setting Eva's holy death up as promoting social reform, Stowe blurred the lines between private and public actions in ways that also claimed the role of author-reformer for herself through her novel's most saint-like female character.

Eliza's rush across an icy Ohio River and her pleas for assistance to travel even further north provided another of the most dramatic – and self-consciously sentimental – episodes in Stowe's text. Here Stowe astutely capitalized on her own and her first audience's anticipated familiarity with abolitionist-supported stories of escaped slaves – including well-known non-fiction accounts that made purposeful appeals to sentimental, body-oriented identification with pain and suffering.[24] But Stowe also revised the familiar plotline of runaways' escapes by emphasizing that, with the Fugitive Slave Act in force, Eliza and Harry are still not safe once they cross from Kentucky into Ohio. She could count on her readers to understand both the old and new geography of the river-crossing moment – its long-held associations with freedom and its diminished force with the 1850 legal change.

If the wild chase was crafted to get her readers' pulses pounding, the succeeding scene at the home of a midwestern US senator and his wife was astutely managed to take advantage of many sentimentalist techniques. When Mary Bird, the kind "little woman" of this chapter, wants to persuade her husband John to ignore the law he apparently helped pass and, instead, to assist Eliza's escape, she appeals to his "heart" as "better than [his] head, in this case." Tellingly, the debate over an escaped slave is held this time in "the parlor," with the skilled domestic orator seated "in her little rocking-chair before the fire," rather than in the halls of Congress. That she prevails is due in large part to the pull of sentimental identification. The senator may be a law-making politician, aware of what he is legally charged to do in this case; yet he is also, as Stowe's chapter title confirms, "but a man." As a man, his thoughts are drawn to family feelings, including touching memories of his own lost son, symbolized in the "drawer full of things – of – of – poor little Henry" (*UTC*, pp. 153, 151).

When the senator suggests that Harry be given some of Henry's clothes, Stowe's readers would have recognized how fully his wife's argument had been won through an appeal to feeling over reason, feminized sentiment over the male-made law. Reading this sequence critically today, we should also recognize the way that Mrs Bird emerges as the pivotal agent guiding the senator's decision and thus, ultimately, saving Eliza and Harry. For Stowe, and presumably for her readers, the true site of social power is the white middle-class woman, using moral suasion to rule the nation.

This scene in the senator's home was crucial to Stowe's marshalling of sentimentalism to her anti-slavery cause and to her positioning of the national political crisis of slavery in a domestic framework. In literary terms, Stowe was making effective rhetorical use of "sentimental materialism," an approach wherein "domestic material culture is represented in great detail and in which personal possessions are endowed with psychological or characterological import."[25] Here, everything from the rocking chair to the fireside to the drawer of little Henry's treasured belongings is charged with intense feeling, leading readers to identify with the white family and, subsequently, with the Birds' support of Eliza and her son.

The victory of the senator's decision to help Eliza and Harry reach freedom is, of course, bigger than the individual case. Promoting a sentimentalized interaction with the human beings Eliza and Harry over abstract conceptions from secular law, Mrs Bird had also won her husband (and presumably the reader) over to a feminized interpretation of the central political issue of the time – the place of slavery in American culture. And at the center of this divine exercise in the literacy of moral suasion is a motherly reading of Biblical text. The senator's revised stance toward the Fugitive Slave Law demonstrates that his wife, who (ironically) claimed that she didn't "know anything about politics," has successfully asserted her moral directives over the legal text he at first had tried to impose (*UTC*, p. 144).

In that vein, Stowe was drawing quite extensively throughout the novel upon a specialized literary genre associated with the ideology of sentimental moral suasion – the American domestic literacy narrative. Domestic literacy narratives portrayed mothers and mother figures teaching children and other childlike characters to read and, through that learning process, to understand the world. The core assumption behind domestic literacy narratives was the idea that mothers managing literacy in the domestic sphere prepared leaders who exercised influence beyond the home.

Stowe's gender-based assertion of this ideal is made quite clear in her depictions of individual female characters in the novel, such as Mrs Shelby, Eva, and Ophelia, as well as in the cumulative impact of their influence on others. While Stowe's treatment of black masculinity in *Uncle Tom's Cabin* was and remains a cause of anxiety among many readers, her portrayal of feminized influence through sentimental pedagogical strategies has offered an alternative focus of interpretation organized around female characters' moral power. Implicit in a number of feminist readings of *Uncle Tom's Cabin* is the suggestion that Stowe had great faith in women's ability to shape the national agenda through moral leadership.[26]

Even in the earliest chapters of the novel, we can see Stowe beginning to develop an argument for women's social influence in her sympathetic construction of Mrs Shelby, mother of young George and kindly mistress of Eliza and Tom. Besides actively resisting the sale of Tom and Harry, Mrs Shelby helps engineer Eliza's successful escape. More importantly, if less directly evident in the plot, she is the maternal teacher behind the enlightened stance George Shelby takes toward the blacks whose well-being he eventually seeks to ensure at the end of the narrative. George Shelby's role as a liberator is, as we have already noted, based on a patronizing stance, but, for Stowe's readers, its grounding in maternally directed values would have been commendable.

Mrs Shelby's influence over George and, through him, over the future of the nation is emphasized in a scene of instruction very early in the narrative, when we first meet Tom. (Stowe's choice of the name "George" for both the

Shelby and Harris heroes is probably not accidental, given domestic literacy narratives' regular exaltation of George Washington and his mother as the ultimate role models for Americans. Even in Tom's humble cabin, after all, there is a picture of the first president.) By teaching Tom to read, George Shelby is both breaking a secular law against slave literacy and endorsing a higher spiritual law affirming Tom's humanity – two actions he surely would not have taken on without the feminized training of his mother. In a complicated image of George listening to Tom's reading efforts, Stowe both infantalizes her title character – by depicting his child-like difficulty "mastering" the text – and holds out a promise of his someday acquiring social power – by echoing other domestic literacy narratives' portraying instruction of young white males who would ultimately gain authority through literacy.

Resonating with scenes from foundational texts of the genre by British authors such as Anna Laetitia Barbauld, Maria Edgeworth and Hannah More, Stowe's depiction of this reading lesson would have also called to mind similar episodes in numerous texts by American writers like Lydia Maria Child, Catharine Maria Sedgwick, and Lydia Sigourney. Highlighting coded elements in this scene, Stowe's language would also provide accessible signs to readers of her day that Tom was acquiring both text-based literacy and broader life skills through this reading lesson, including a brand of enlightened Christian masculinity. In granting this important learning experience to Tom, Stowe was affirming his potential – and through him the capabilities of other black males – in ways that her initial reading audience would have easily recognized, especially since they would have been encountering parallel domestic literacy narratives with similar story-lines in the pages of the *Era* at the same time.

Interestingly, by having George assume the role of teacher that was typically fulfilled by mothers in most versions of the genre, Stowe took several strategic steps toward making the radical components of her argument palatable to her audience. She avoided the potentially troubling scene of an adult white woman interacting intimately with a black man in a one-on-one reading lesson; and she held out the hope that white males like George could enact moral leadership in the public sphere based on their mothers' teaching in the home. In addition, she placed Tom, her central black male character, in a situation blending acknowledgment of his potential (he is learning to read, after all) with reinforcement of his limits (he remains dependent upon George's knowledge and the choice to share it). Meanwhile, for her own first readers, the "real" source of power in this scene would nonetheless have been obvious – the mother Mrs Shelby, off-stage but still the influence shaping the actions of both her son and Tom.

Later, Tom's education is taken over by Eva St Clare, whose gentle teaching again echoes the familiar storyline of domestic literacy narratives in antebellum America. The cultural force of this recurring scene and the ideology behind it have been repeatedly confirmed by the illustrations of Tom and Eva reading together, an image so often included in editions of *Uncle Tom's Cabin*.[27] Like the episode of George teaching Tom, the occasions of Eva's instruction are also strategically conceived to avoid what might otherwise have been disquieting to Stowe's readers – the idea of a young white female teaching an adult black male lessons that could provide an avenue to social power.

Frederick Douglass's report of his master's angry order to his young mistress to stop giving Douglass reading lessons is telling in this regard. As Stowe herself outlined in *A Key to Uncle Tom's Cabin*, Douglass's master "forbade" the lessons, on grounds of its being "unlawful" to "to teach a slave to read" but, more importantly, because it was "unsafe": "if you teach that nigger . . . how to read, there would be no keeping him. It would forever unfit him to be a slave. He would at once become unmanageable, and of no value to his master."[28]

Over time, one way Americans worked to contain this potentially subversive scenario of the young white girl Eva's instructing a black man was by re-casting Uncle Tom – in illustrations, in dramatic stagings, and in shared memory – as an elderly "uncle" rather than a strong middle-aged figure. But even in her original 1850s printed text, Stowe was already careful to revise the bedrock scene of domestic literacy narratives to avoid deploying too much power in Tom's direction. Eva, who is significantly also named "Evangeline," focuses on spiritual, not secular, instruction. A child herself, she can mimic some of the literacy lessons mothers taught to young white boys, but her version of the familiar curriculum of domestic literacy narratives is limited. Advanced as she is in terms of spiritual development, she will never mature to worldly adulthood, so she and Tom, though reading intimately together, pose no threat to the status quo of white social dominance. By the time of Eva's sentimental death, she has taught Tom all she knows and, from Stowe's perspective, that is enough. Bounded in by Eva-inculcated Biblical injunctions calling for patient suffering, Tom has learned to embody a religiously sanctioned and feminized black manhood that asserts his humanity (and, by extension, that of all slaves) without threatening Stowe's white readers.

The bond that develops between Ophelia and Topsy offers a fascinating echo of the teacher–student relationships between George and Tom and between Eva and Tom. The efforts of George Shelby and Eva St Clare to facilitate Tom's literacy development reiterate many other antebellum domestic literacy narratives, which often depicted well-taught white middle-class children benevolently extending their learning to others less fortunate than themselves. Another variation on the mother-teaching-child plotline was the story of a single woman managing the literacy acquisition of others' children, either in a school setting or as a maiden aunt or kindly neighbor teaching in a domestic environment. (Fictional examples include Sarah Hale's "The Village Schoolmistress," Lydia Sigourney's "Margaret Mercer," Lydia Maria Child's "Louisa Preston," and Catharine Maria Sedgwick's "Old Maids"). Stowe's Ophelia enacts this pattern, which claimed a meaningful maternal role in society for single women like Stowe's sister Catharine Beecher, whose own writings also contributed to this ideology.

Stowe may even have had her sister Catharine in mind when envisioning the character of Ophelia, the Yankee cousin of Augustine St Clare. Catharine and Ophelia have much in common, including a commitment to New England values but some difficulty acting on those views; sharp intelligence but a limited capacity for generous feelings; and an impressive self-confidence but intolerance for others' failings. Stowe's affectionately satirical tone in her early descriptions of Ophelia is noteworthy, and so is her choice to depict Ophelia's shortcomings as more representative than unique.

Though we can certainly mount the same critique of Topsy's consignment to Africa as we have already outlined in relation to George Harris's emigration, we should acknowledge the progressive components in the Ophelia–Topsy storyline, especially Stowe's insistence that the northern white women represented by Ophelia need to reform. Stowe's pressure on Ophelia's failings stands in as a larger critique of many northerners' inadequate responses to slavery up to this time, just as Ophelia's personal reformation offers a map for others to follow. In a text that presents the appealing southern mistress Mrs Shelby as well as the unfeeling Marie St Clare, Stowe surely deserves some credit for providing some range in her northern women characters as well. She balances her idealized treatment of Rachel Halliday, the Quaker guardian of runaways like the Harrises, with the more complex and dynamic portrait of Miss Ophelia. After all, as St Clare points out, when we first meet her, Ophelia is quite ready to fault southerners for owning slaves, but has no desire to "kiss" (i.e., feel genuine affection for) a black person herself. Similarly, she donates to foreign missions, but fails to support needy slaves at home. Having begun teaching Topsy in response to her cousin's well-placed barbs, Ophelia is unsuccessful until she shifts her methods from punishment to affection.[29] Eventually, influenced by Eva's example of sentimental pedagogy, Ophelia is ready to direct Topsy's continued instruction in the north and to adopt the child, whom she now truly loves. Thus, the sub-plot Stowe designs around the education of Topsy is equally about the re-education of Ophelia – her gradual assumption of an enlightened maternal didactic role. And, in depicting the making of a new Ophelia, Stowe was also demonstrating the need for a more activist anti-slavery, pro-black stance among the white women in her audience.

Indeed, taken together, the southern and northern maternal teacher figures Mrs Shelby and Ophelia highlight both the limits and the potential of the social role they embody for 1850s America. Neither of these would-be social agents is successful in their efforts to save Tom. Mrs Shelby's pleas to her husband's moral sense go unheeded, and Ophelia's letter to the Shelbys arrives too late to effect his rescue from Legree. However, both motherly teachers do exercise influence, from Stowe's perspective, on the long-term health of the nation through their management of children who can be leaders for a more utopian future. Mrs Shelby's teaching of her son guides him toward his liberator role. Ophelia's teaching of Topsy prepares the young black girl for Christian mission service.

Significantly, Stowe also imagines the possibility of black women becoming maternal leaders – but not necessarily all black women. As a number of critics have observed, in contrast to affirming depictions of such mulatta characters as Eliza, Cassy and Emmeline, Stowe's emphasis on authorizing women as active agents in American culture is not fully extended to include the "pure" black women in the novel. Though perhaps less overtly offensive than the stereotypes invoked for Sam, Andy, and Adolph, Stowe's portrayals of characters like Dinah, the St. Clares' cook, are nonetheless quite efficient at containing them in ways not applied to the mixed-race figures like Eliza Harris.

Meanwhile, however, by underscoring educative activities that figures like Ophelia and Mrs Shelby have in common, and, most specifically, in the letter that passes between these two women near the novel's end, Stowe signaled to her first readers a strategy for cross-regional alliances through which white middle-class women (her primary audience) could unite against slavery's evils – and ultimately for a reclamation of the national landscape grounded in feminized moral suasion. When we read *Uncle Tom's Cabin* as a domestic literacy narrative, the agency these two central motherly teachers gain by educating George Shelby and Topsy becomes very clear, serving as a potential pattern to replicate, whether in the south or the north.

A focus on Ophelia and Mrs Shelby as points of identification for Stowe's first audience also compensates for readings that have concentrated almost exclusively on Eva St Clare. The death of "little Eva" is surely one of the novel's most striking episodes, a plot development played out using sentimentalism's most tried-and-true tools. Indeed, we know from readers' records of their engagement with *Uncle Tom's Cabin* that many have found this episode particularly touching. We also know, though, as Richard Wright and others have pointed out, that moving readers to tears does not guarantee they will be moved to social action. The very tears a figure like Eva generates may even obscure more proactive aspects of a narrative argument. With that in mind, we may develop a more nuanced view of sentimentalism's cultural work by calling attention to the novel's mother figures and not just its angelic white child.

From periodical serial into book form

While *Uncle Tom's Cabin* was still unfolding in the *National Era*, Stowe was already preparing to bring out the book. Beecher family members had a number of contacts in the publishing world, so those were the first firms considered. Catharine, as usual, tried to take charge. She had been living with the Stowes for the stated purpose of relieving her sister of household cares during the serial's composition. Family correspondence suggests she may not have been the most enthusiastic baby-sitter. But she was eager to guide the publication process – both early on and later – since she had authored a number of books herself. She first attempted to negotiate with her publisher, Phillips, Sampson, and Company. This group politely rejected Stowe's manuscript, based on the limited appeal of past anti-slavery narratives, but also out of deference to their southern clientele.

Stowe had better luck with the Boston firm of John Jewett, whose wife had been avidly reading the installments in the *Era*. As Gamaliel Bailey had been for the serial version, Jewett probably seemed a very good fit for the book. Jewett had handled books by Stowe's younger brother, Henry Ward Beecher, and by her father Lyman Beecher. Furthermore, Jewett was known for publishing religious texts – an indication, perhaps, of how Stowe and her family were viewing *Uncle Tom's Cabin* prior to its entering the market.[30]

Jewett's first edition of *Uncle Tom's Cabin* appeared on 20 March 1852. While there is some variation across sources in the tallying, there is no question that the book was an immediate success way beyond anyone's expectations. Sales were in the thousands right away, and in the hundreds of thousands in short order. Thousands of copies were sold the first day, and second printing was already in the works within weeks. Fifty thousand copies were sold in the US within two months of the book's initial publication, and a million and a half had been printed within the year.[31] Significantly, these figures do not even take into account the astounding success the book would have overseas. Particularly in England, Stowe's novel became an immediate sensation.

As Bailey had done for the serial, Jewett both reported an enthusiastic response to the text and stoked sales to higher levels. His account of three paper mills running night and day, power presses working round the clock, and book binders stitching madly to keep up with demand became a familiar part of the legend of the book's popularity. Certainly, demand was unprecedented for an anti-slavery publication, and sales bred more sales. While publications like Susan Warner's *The Wide, Wide World* and Maria Cummins's *The Lamplighter* had already proven that women's novels could be bestsellers in America, Stowe's text generated similar sales levels much faster than such predecessors. Before the year had ended, Jewett produced both a more expensive edition of *Uncle Tom's Cabin* with an array of illustrations for the holiday gift market and a cheaper edition aimed at the masses. Both of these sold rapidly.

Harriet and Calvin Stowe were quite surprised and excited by their new-found income. The first royalty payment alone, delivered several months after initial publication, totaled over $10,000, a remarkable sum at the time. Although Stowe had already published her geography text book and her collection of sketches written in Cincinnati (*The Mayflower*), neither venture had been particularly lucrative. So, based on her prior experience, she could not have anticipated the windfall from her first novel, despite its popularity as a serial.

Meanwhile, given the enormous sales *Uncle Tom's Cabin* was achieving, some friends and family – especially the ever-officious Catharine – urged Harriet to re-negotiate with Jewett. Catharine and Calvin were both trying to manage the business affairs in the beginning, and they were not always in agreement. Catharine arranged a half-and-half arrangement with Jewett before publication, by which he and Harriet would have split revenues after all expenses, only to have Calvin step into the discussions before that contract was signed. The two men then came to terms at 10 percent royalty, after Calvin pulled back from requesting 20 percent, which Jewett declared he could not afford. Between the first agreement and the final one, Catharine was away on a trip, and when she returned to discover the new terms, she was furious, especially once sales piled up. Calvin, in contrast, reported being highly pleased with the burgeoning income from the book and follow-up publishing projects that Jewett was handling (such as *A Key to Uncle Tom's Cabin*, a German translation of *Uncle Tom's Cabin*, and a children's edition). Harriet stayed above the fray for awhile. She wrote to her brother Edward, defending Jewett from Catharine's complaints and celebrating the energetic (and costly) efforts her publisher had made to promote the book. In the same letter, however, she indicated that she was not planning to retain Jewett as her publisher indefinitely, and she attributed her plans to change both to his stubborn negotiations over royalties and to his tiresome personality. By 1854, she had made Phillips, Sampson, and Company – the firm that had originally turned down *Uncle Tom's Cabin* – her publisher for new projects, though Jewett still maintained rights to her first novel.[32]

In between the initial edition of *Uncle Tom's Cabin* and Stowe's affiliation with a different publisher, she carried out another proprietary move demonstrating that, Charles Stowe's protestations about her inexperience aside, she was quite willing to seek control over her writing as a financial enterprise. In 1853, she filed a copyright infringement suit against F. W. Thomas, a printer whose Philadelphia-based newspaper *Die Freie Presse* had brought out an unauthorized translation of *Uncle Tom's Cabin* for the fairly substantial German-speaking readership then in the US. Even though Stowe lost her case, this effort to expand the rights of authorship in America still represented a watershed in legal and literary history.[33]

Stowe's attempt to regulate publication of her novel in a way not previously recognized by custom or law marked her increasingly determined management of *Uncle Tom's Cabin* as a commodity – a professional publication that affirmed her talent as author, her rights as creator to control its continued circulation, and her ongoing access to income from the work. Significantly, Stowe initiated her suit over a version of *Uncle Tom's Cabin* that stood to cost her a clear loss in income, since her then-publisher John Jewett had taken on an authorized German translation project that would be in competition with Thomas's. At a time when play versions of the novel were already being produced and a growing range of memorabilia was being sold, not to mention pirated editions being circulated in England, Stowe tried to expand her ability to reap financial benefits from her book in the domain most directly connected to her writing itself – a text circulating in print form within the US. Thus, *Stowe v. Thomas*, like her family's efforts to re-negotiate her arrangements with Jewett, indicated that she had made a decided transition beyond the relatively amateurish role of gendered authorship she had learned through magazine writing, participation in Cincinnati's Semicolon Club, and the didactic projects she had generated collaboratively with Catharine. By 1853, managing the property of *Uncle Tom's Cabin* had made Harriet Beecher Stowe a self-consciously professional author.

In 1860, Stowe made several more moves showing that she was no longer naïve about the business end of publishing. While traveling in Italy, she had become friends with James Fields and his wife Annie, whose parlor at 148 Charles Street in Boston was a center of literary culture. Having rearranged her plans for traveling home in June, 1860, so as to sail on the same ship as the Fieldses and the family of Nathaniel Hawthorne, Stowe used the voyage to cultivate what would become a pivotal relationship with Annie and her husband. As Mrs Fields later recalled, the two-week voyage was "beautiful," with Stowe frequently joining Hawthorne's wife Sophia, the Fieldses and others on deck to tell stories "of New England life and her early experiences." Although some have described Hawthorne as less drawn to such socializing than others on board, Annie Fields reported that he enthusiastically declared one day: "Oh, . . . I wish we might never get there," i.e., home to the US (*Life and Letters*, pp. 282–83).

Stowe certainly spent this time aboard ship to her advantage. Fields was assuming the editorship of the *Atlantic*, then the most prestigious periodical for literature in the US, and he was a partner in the well-known Boston firm of Ticknor and Fields, publisher of such esteemed American writers as Hawthorne and Ralph Waldo Emerson. By this point, Stowe was a savvy enough manager of her own career to recognize the benefits of having such a prominent group take over future publishing of *Uncle Tom's Cabin*. So, when Jewett shut down his business later that summer, the plates for the novel were transferred over to Fields's firm. Over time, Ticknor and Fields would publish numerous other books by Stowe, nurturing a career that remained rooted in the values of *Uncle Tom's Cabin* while also adding new dimensions.

Earlier on, while the ink on its book edition was barely dry, *Uncle Tom's Cabin* began generating a vast array of other texts, and it has continued to do so, on into the twenty-first century. Seemingly overnight, the figure of Uncle Tom – often with Eva and/or Topsy – appeared on widely diverse nineteenth-century products, in the US and in Europe. From statuettes to wallpaper, from sheet music to paintings and dishware, what today would be called "tie-ins" exploded into an early form of mass marketing. Even today, the "Uncle Tom" construct remains readily available, whether as a derisive put-down in conversation or a resonating element in new artistic productions. The book's narrative has been re-cast, excerpted, and parodied in a plethora of literary forms, from melodrama to song lyrics, juvenile re-tellings to translations. In a sense, this never-ending generation of new versions of *Uncle Tom's Cabin* claims a persistent creative power for Stowe, thereby raising intriguing questions about authorship as a social process. To what extent is Stowe a kind of co-author for such texts? To what extent is her narrative itself exercising a kind of redoubtable authorial energy? In that vein, one explanation behind the resurgence of interest in Stowe's career over the last decades of the twentieth century lies in how much the rewritings of her work demonstrate principles of poststructuralism and postmodernism, including views of language's abiding cultural power, of authorship as a vexed site of social action, and of discourse as multifaceted.

For the virtually countless texts that owe debts to *Uncle Tom's Cabin*, sorting out the blends ranging between original authorship with a bit of strategic allusiveness (as in Richard Wright's *Uncle Tom's Children*), on the one hand, and appropriation with limited new material (as in several of the unapproved translations), on the other, could easily produce more than a book's worth of analysis. On a case-by-case basis, we would find varying degrees of dependency versus cooptation – situations where we could argue that Stowe's work was (unfairly and extensively) appropriated against her will, but also occasions when the now-broadly-shared cultural capital of *Uncle Tom's Cabin* has been reconfigured to striking new effect. Had she never written another book, merely on the basis of *Uncle Tom's Cabin*'s wide-ranging adaptations and extensions, Stowe could be viewed as a highly prolific author.

Stowe's *Key, Dred,* and *The Christian Slave*

We can certainly criticize Stowe for taking over the life experiences of African Americans like the former slave Josiah Henson to serve her own writerly needs. But we should also see that her own ability to maintain control over the textual property of *Uncle Tom's Cabin*, Uncle Tom, and other elements within her original narrative was severely limited in her own day by the lack of a strong international copyright, and also by constraining views of gendered authorship's place in world culture. Indeed, acquisitive as she was of others' materials, Stowe actually gained very little, in direct monetary terms, from the vast textual production emerging in the novel's wake. She certainly wasn't equipped – as a Disney executive would be today – to regulate a corporate empire based on the sustained appeal of her most popular literary product. Nonetheless, as an increasingly savvy professional, Stowe did capitalize on the success of her first novel with several other publications in the 1850s.

Three of Stowe's post-*Uncle Tom's Cabin* writings built directly on the success of her first novel. *A Key to Uncle Tom's Cabin*; her second anti-slavery novel, *Dred*; and the dramatic production of *The Christian Slave* all encouraged audiences' continued fascination with her identity as an anti-slavery author. Taken together, these works indicate Stowe's strong awareness of the special place that *Uncle Tom's Cabin* was claiming in American culture and her wish to direct that ongoing process. Furthermore, by commanding sizeable audiences, these extensions of *Uncle Tom's Cabin* also helped solidify her position as a literary figure to be reckoned with, both at home and abroad.

A Key to Uncle Tom's Cabin

Even as the early press runs for the book version of *Uncle Tom's Cabin* were being snatched up in America and Europe, Stowe was already at work on her *Key*, a hybrid expository text defending her first anti-slavery book against charges mounted by pro-slavery opponents. To write the *Key*, Stowe called upon family members and friends for assistance, assembling material from a wide array of sources. The result, as Cindy Weinstein has observed, was "an irate and ironic critique of critiques of *Uncle Tom's Cabin*" through arguments seeking "to prove the mutual exclusivity of being both pro-slavery and sympathetic."[34]

Stowe realized that defending her novel would require presenting evidence for the anti-slavery claims she had made there. But it would also entail showing that she herself was worthy of trust from readers, while her attackers were devoid of the very Christian principles central to American life. Her two-pronged counterattack was cleverly conceived, because the assaults on *Uncle Tom's Cabin* had sought to discredit the book as a false depiction of slavery, but also to paint Stowe herself as an unwomanly violator of accepted social norms, and therefore personally unreliable. (See Chapter 4 for a fuller discussion of 1850s responses to Stowe's novel.)

Her use of the word "*Key*" in the title could hardly have been an accident, in this regard. With this metaphor as her core term, Stowe suggested, she was freely opening up her work to the full scrutiny that only a trustworthy story and author could stand. The full subtitle of the *Key* is also quite telling, declaring that Stowe's new work would be "*presenting the original facts and documents upon which the story* [of *Uncle Tom's Cabin*] *is founded; together with corroborative statements verifying the truth of the work.*" As pivotal words such as "facts," "documents," "corroborative," and "verifying" indicate, Stowe's second anti-slavery text was designed at virtually a word-by-word level to bolster the authenticity of her first book. Having been accused of all manner of exaggeration – even fabrication – in *Uncle Tom's Cabin*, Stowe piled up detailed refutations against such charges. To do so necessitated a complex rhetorical dance, positioning an admittedly novelistic text as being entirely grounded in fact.

Stowe set the stage with an introductory salvo against her critics. Like her subtitle, her preface repeatedly invoked the language of non-fiction and documentation to situate *Uncle Tom's Cabin* within a context of unassailable, fact-based authority:

> In fictitious writing, it is possible to find refuge from the hard and the terrible, by inventing scenes and characters of a more pleasing nature. No such resource is open in a work of fact; and the subject of this work [*Uncle Tom's Cabin* and, by extension, this new *Key*] is one on which the truth, if told at all, must needs be very dreadful. There is no bright side to slavery, as such. . . . The writer has aimed, as far as possible, to say what is true, and only that, without regard to the effect which it may have upon any persons or party. She hopes that what she has said will be examined without bitterness, – in that serious and earnest spirit which is appropriate for the examination of so very serious a subject. It would be vain for her to indulge the hope of being wholly free from error. In the wide field which she has been called to go over, there is a possibility of many mistakes. She can only say that she has used the most honest and earnest endeavors to learn the truth. (*Key*, p. iii)

The language of Stowe's preface is calculating in its seeming transparency. She starts off with a purportedly straightforward contrast between "fictitious writing" and the "work of fact," claiming that the former is allowed to use invention to make "scenes and characters . . . more pleasing" but that the latter must stick to "the truth." She assumes *a priori* that *Uncle Tom's Cabin* would fall into the second category – being a work of straightforward "truth" – rather than the first; that is, she avoids addressing the potentially thorny problem of what might be a blurred genre identity – a blend of "fictitious writing" with "fact" in a novelistic text – by pretending that such hybridity would always be out of the question. She proceeds to relate her novel's supposedly fact-based genre identity with its serious subject – slavery – a topic to which, she says, "There is not a bright side." Given slavery's unique position as an ultra-serious topic, in other words, no honest reporter would ever stop short of the full, though "dreadful," truth. Stowe's finessing the implicit questions about genre categories' connections to reliability issues is understandable, given the relatively unsettled status of such terms in the 1850s. However, her claim that a narrative like *Uncle Tom's Cabin* can be assessed in terms of its "truthfulness" by comparing it to real-life sources is also quite strategic rhetorically.

Stowe then moves to a discreetly veiled charge against her attackers, as "[s]he hopes that what she has said will be examined without bitterness." Of course, Stowe is fully aware that her novel has already aroused much "bitterness," so her ironic plea here is really for a change in behavior, one which she suggests could generate a "serious and earnest" spirit of shared analysis. By marshalling this verbal irony, Stowe is saying that those who have assaulted her work have, up to now, exhibited a stance quite the opposite of "serious and earnest," one which, as a textual manager trying to re-direct their reading and response, she now aims to reform. Stowe is again being strategic: though it is highly unlikely she can change the opinion of her attackers, by pretending to view them as worthy partners in search of truth, she makes it more likely that readers who have been uncertain about her work up to now will be persuaded that she is herself "earnest" and trustworthy.

As is so often the case in Stowe's writing, what she then presents as if an afterthought is actually a central element in her argument. Proposing "It would be vain . . . to indulge in the hope of being wholly free from error," Stowe heads off in advance what might otherwise have been a vulnerable point to assail. Go ahead, she allows, find stray errors in this new defense of *Uncle Tom's Cabin* as a dependable depiction of slavery's ills. Such slips will be fruitless to cite in any counter-counter-attack, since "[i]n the wide field which she has been called to go over," there are bound to be "many mistakes." What counts, Stowe asserts, is the preponderance of her evidence and, most importantly, the "honest and earnest" stance she has cultivated, seeking "to learn the truth."

After laying this careful groundwork in her preface, Stowe cites evidence designed to demonstrate both her own reliability as a researcher-reporter for *Uncle Tom's Cabin* and, by extension, the inappropriateness of any attempts to discredit her. She presents her argument in four parts, gathering cumulative force from both the quantity of evidence assembled and the confidence maintained in her tone.

In Part I, she concentrates on providing explanatory sketches for important characters in the novel, offering evidence in each case of how the figures had been drawn to match real-life types and actual experiences. Characters reviewed in this section are presented roughly in the order in which a reader would have encountered them in the novel. By noting the evidence she offers in each case, we can infer specific points of attack that had been made against the characters. Haley, the Shelbys, George Harris, Eliza, Tom, Miss Ophelia, the St Clares (Marie and her husband), Legree, Topsy, and "the Quakers" all claim her attention. Embedded in her defense of her characterizations are references to real-life parallels, alongside certifications of her sources.

For example, in revisiting the character of Tom, Stowe quotes from the preface a certain Bishop Meade had written for "a little book, entitled, 'Sketches of Old Virginia Servants.'" Stowe uses both Meade's description of pious, loyal slaves in the "Sketches" and the trustworthy identity of Meade himself to support her depiction of Tom in the novel. Similarly, to defend herself against criticism that she had painted Simon Legree in excessively cruel terms, Stowe cites the firsthand observations of plantation life by a number of authorities, including "the Rev. Mr. Barrows, now officiating as teacher of Hebrew in Andover Theological Seminary." She recounts Barrows's conversation with a "gentleman" the reverend met "while at New Orleans," a southerner who verified that plantations there came in two models: enlightened establishments with "abundant provision" as well as "moral and religious instruction" for slaves, versus "the opposite system," which Barrows's informant said was being practiced at a nearby plantation. Clearly framing these portrayals as a parallel to the contrast between St Clare's and Legree's homes in the novel, Stowe highlights Reverend Barrows's first-hand view of the Legree stand-in, a plantation where "the woe-struck, dejected aspect of its laborers fully confirmed" the cruelty of its master (*Key*, pp. 24, 41–2).

Part II begins with charges critics have made against her and *Uncle Tom's Cabin*. She then refutes the charges by using legal references, including material from both Hebrew (Biblical) and Roman law. Besides affirming the veracity of *Uncle Tom's Cabin*, this section also argues implicitly for Stowe's skill and reliability as a researcher of fact. In more than one instance, Stowe exhibits her own trustworthiness by pretending to take seriously a complaint that had been lodged against her, then demolishing the accusation through astute analysis of legal texts. She reports that the *Courier & Enquirer* had cited the case of *Souther v. The Commonwealth of Virginia* as evidence of falsity in her episode of Legree's torturing Tom to death. Declaring that this critique had prompted her to re-think the probability of Tom's being killed in the way her novel portrayed, Stowe says she "accordingly took the pains to procure a report of the case, designing to publish it as an offset to the many barbarities which research into this branch of the subject obliges one to unfold." Instead, Stowe then takes pains to illustrate, a full review of the case and its appeal actually must lead anyone with true Christian sympathy – and the basic ability to read – to amazement at how the "lawyers calmly sat and examined, and cross-examined, on particulars [of cruelty] known before only in the records of the Inquisition." Stowe mounts a similar sally against "the Revised Statutes of North Carolina" that clearly allow for the killing of slaves, and she cites evidence of the application of the statutes in a Wilmington case as recent as 1850, the timeframe for Tom's story. Throughout this section, Stowe repeatedly uses the word "protection" ironically, first presenting information on southern laws that purport to offer slaves some legal protection, then revealing the hollowness behind such claims (*Key*, pp. 79, 71, 83–5).

Part III extends this theme of fallacious "protection" to argue that, sadly, slaves cannot even count on the right feelings Stowe had sought to cultivate in *Uncle Tom's Cabin*. Here Stowe shifts the ground of her argument from the narrowly legal to the moral. For instance, she invites her readers to "Suppose the slave-law were enacted with regard to all the Irish in our country, and they were parcelled off as the property of any man who had money enough to buy them. Suppose their right to vote, their right to bring suit in any case, their right to bear testimony in courts of justice, their right to contract a legal marriage, their right to hold property or to make contracts of any sort, were all by one stroke of law blotted out." In a continuing litany of "suppose" scenarios, Stowe proceeds to apply to "Irishmen" all the inhumane constraints associated with enslavement of blacks, including denial of opportunities for learning, as well as abuses ranging up to beating and murder (*Key*, p. 126).

Having confirmed through this "suppose" comparison the basic inhuman-ity at the heart of slavery, Stowe lays out a long series of examples of slavery's inhumanity in real-life practice, thereby refuting charges against her novel as exaggerating abuses against slaves. By referencing actual advertisements for slave sales, published calls for the return of runaways (often including physical descriptions with signs of past abuse, such as brandings), specific information on estate distributions, and more legal cases, Stowe assembles extensive evidence to shore up *Uncle Tom's Cabin* and to characterize her critics as inherently untrustworthy, and inhumane to boot.

Stowe's final counter-attack in Part IV marshals irony and near-compulsive documentation. Here, though, the author expands her battleground considerably by highlighting the failures of the Christian Church in the south to fight against slavery. Asserting "There is no country in the world where the religious influence has a greater ascendancy than in America," Stowe feigns amazement that the "influence of the clergy" has not successfully wiped out slavery already. Here, though she had in her own preface urged her opponents to avoid "bitterness" in their ongoing dialogue, Stowe violates her own rule, as she bemoans the ways in which "the Southern clergy and the church . . . can tolerate and encourage acts of lawless violence, and risk all the dangers of encouraging mob law" for the sake of slavery. Characterizing slavery as "a simple retrogression of society to the worse abuses of the middle ages," she is, of course, also positioning the south as a backward culture, so that any attempt by a so-called "religious man, born and educated at the South" to be a true Christian is surely doomed to failure as long as slavery exists. Calling on the example of Christ and the authority of the Bible, Stowe challenges her opponents to recognize the essential injustice of slavery in religious terms. Her certainty that Christ will condemn both the slaveholder and the slave supporter is clear in her final sentences, anticipating "the last judgement," when the Lord "shall say unto you, 'Inasmuch as ye have done it to the least of these, my brethren, ye have done it unto me'" (*Key*, pp. 193, 203, 256).

Dred: A tale of the Great Dismal Swamp

If *A Key to Uncle Tom's Cabin* offered a forceful rejoinder to those criticizing *Uncle Tom's Cabin* as biased against the southern slaveholder, then *Dred* can be read as Stowe's extended answer to another group of critics. Stowe's second anti-slavery novel addressed the concerns of those who, even in her own day, had found her depiction of blacks' future in America excessively limited and her recommendations to anti-slavery activists too timid.[35] In this case, rather than an ironic riposte, she revised her own earlier position. And at the heart of this more radical statement on slavery is a new title character – one far more righteously aggressive than Tom had been. In *Dred*, Stowe limns a black leader ready to demand freedom for himself, and also to claim it for others. In the community Dred establishes beyond the reach of plantation culture, we see a hero for this life, rather than a martyr awaiting salvation in heaven.

Like its more famous forerunner, which responded to the Fugitive Slave Law of 1850, the 1856 anti-slavery novel *Dred* may also have been prompted by specific events in the ongoing north/south political conflict in the United States. In this case, passage of the 1854 Kansas–Nebraska Act allowed for the introduction of slavery into the western territories, thus making Kansas a major site of conflict; proponents and opponents of slavery struggled to gain adherents there, eventually leading to the violent episodes known as "bleeding Kansas." Also, Stowe may not have initially christened her title character after the Dred of the *Dred Scott v. Sandford* case, which was already brewing as she was writing, but she would have appreciated the resonances in their names, and she was quite straightforward in depicting her new black male hero as inspired more by Nat Turner and Denmark Vessey than by the suffering, Christ-like martyr she had associated with Tom.[36] Though its conclusion has some of the same ambivalence as in the earlier novel, *Dred* and its title character are far more ready to support violent resistance to slavery's abuses than Tom had been.

Stowe blends genre features from the plantation novel and African Americans' slave narratives to tell her story. In the first case, she initially establishes the outlines for a marriage plot like those in many plantation novels, but then undermines the anticipated narrative trajectory to demonstrate that the south's underlying cultural value system can no longer hold. In the second case, she uses a strategy of affiliation: borrowing conventions from slave narratives, she affirms the belief systems associated with that genre, including the superiority of moral law over flawed judicial systems and the strength of black leadership and faith in the face of slavery's abuses. In linking these two diverse traditions within one text, she simultaneously revamps the terrain of anti-slavery writing that she had first explored in *Uncle Tom's Cabin*. With its complex accretion of many literary traditions – including Biblical stories, legal cases, minstrelsy, folk tales, and biography, as well as the genres already mentioned – *Dred* is a capacious, allusive and sometimes contradictory text that assumes a high degree of readerly sophistication about literary forms.

Set in the Carolinas, *Dred* begins by laying out the complicated familial relations around Canema, a plantation whose young mistress, Nina Gordon, is dependent upon the administrative skill of Harry Gordon, the able mixed-race manager who (unknown to Nina) is actually her half-brother. Harry is as admirable a figure as his half-brother (and Nina's brother) the white Tom Gordon is despicable. Tom, a loutish drunkard and ruffian, lusts after Harry's wife Lisette and hovers menacingly around the plantation his sister and Harry have collaboratively organized under a sentimental brand of governance. Meanwhile, Nina spends many of the early scenes in the novel caught up in the romantic who-shall-she-marry storyline so familiar to nineteenth-century readers of plantation novels. In a series of episodes that could be read as a beat-them-at-their-own-game response to many southern anti-Tom narratives, Stowe at first focuses on Nina's playful and distinctively immature machinations to juggle multiple suitors.

Gradually, Stowe's young heroine progresses from silly immaturity to an appreciation of Edward Clayton, a serious-minded but appealing suitor whose sister Anne becomes a role model for Nina. Then, in a turning point for Nina's personal growth, Nina visits Magnolia Grove, the Claytons' South Carolina home. Stowe sets up Magnolia Grove as a utopian (if patronizingly benevolent) site of enlightened governance, especially in comparison to the callous attitudes of Nina's brother Tom. As Nina takes in the commitment to educational uplift embodied in Anne Clayton's school for slaves, the novel veers toward a female *bildungsroman* positing Nina's maturation as tied not just to marriage, but also to a new social activism.

At Magnolia Grove, slaves have the benefit of Anne's teaching and Edward's paternal protection, at least until a group of coarse villains egged on by Tom begins to terrorize the more refined and generous whites in the region – burning down the schoolhouse and beating up any leaders who are opposed to the abuse of slaves. More insistently than in *Uncle Tom's Cabin*, Stowe's plantation scenes, replete with kindly, affectionate owners and (relatively) comfortable slaves, are strategically arranged to underscore the inherent dangers behind such a precarious system. For example, she cultivates intense readerly concern by juxtaposing Harry's deep love of Lisette with Tom's evil designs.

Similarly, Stowe has the tender-hearted Nina resist the opportunity to exercise her "rights" to ownership over a Mississippi mulatta (Cora Gordon) who had been married to and emancipated by a Gordon cousin, whose death has now rendered this mother and her children susceptible to claims from any white relative of the dead master. Nina asserts the kind of "feel-right" Christian response touted in *Uncle Tom's Cabin* and seeks to guarantee that vulnerable family's safety. Yet, Stowe's barbed portrayal of the small-minded legal advisor Mr Jekyl, who argues a pro-re-enslavement position in this case, alerts readers that, in this novel, even the most generous stances based in sentimental impulses will be subject to constant assault. Nina appeals to Mr Jekyl's religious sense, reminding him that he is "an elder in the church" who should therefore draw on the Gospel to resist any purported "*right* to take this woman and her children, and her property." But Tom Gordon feels no compunction about claiming Cora Gordon and her children as chattel. "[C]onfound the humbug," Stowe has Tom rant to his sister, "who cares whether it is right or not?" With these ominous revisions of the "feel-right" argument she had presented in

Uncle Tom's Cabin, Stowe prepares her readers for the more violent episodes to come in this novel – from both supporters and opponents of slavery.[37]

Tom's brutal attitude and the threats from his vigilantes are a horrifying counterpoint to the Claytons' benevolent governance, with the mob behavior Tom incites throughout the novel demonstrating the ultimate inability of individual slaveholders (however kind) to maintain a Christian stance in a region where slavery is in force. As in *Uncle Tom's Cabin*, the death of an angelic female foreshadows more losses to come, for Nina Gordon dies a suitably sentimental, holy death after bravely nursing others during an epidemic. Foreclosing her anticipated marriage to Edward, Nina's death signals the impossibility of avoiding the contagion of slavery, even for those aspiring to an enlightened brand of plantation life.

After Nina's death, the novel's focus shifts from the romance plot to a more pointedly political examination of slavery's institutional-level ills. The second half of the novel concentrates on the escalating conflict between Edward Clayton and Nina's brother Tom, who takes advantage of her death to assert his power over the Canema slaves. By focusing on Clayton's inability to defeat such evil in a series of legal cases, Stowe stresses that slavery has corrupted all of southern society.

The first of these legal cases actually takes place early in Volume II, before Nina's death, and it focuses on Milly, an appealing slave woman who is loaned out by the Gordons to work for a white man (a Mr Barker) in a neighboring town. Mr Barker became so infuriated by Milly's brave defense of a slave child who had accidentally stained his clothing that he beat Milly and shot at her. When Milly returns home to Canema to tell Nina this story, her kind mistress quickly contacts Edward Clayton, whose budding law career is soon put to a rough test when he represents Milly in a suit against Barker. Edward's eager defense might seem mainly to reiterate Stowe's understanding that many southerners are good people, determined to serve as protectors of slaves. Indeed, Stowe has Edward observe: "It is a debt which we owe . . . to the character of our state, and to the purity of our institutions, to prove the efficiency of the law in behalf of that class of our population whose helplessness places them more particularly under our protection. They are to us in the condition of children under age; and any violation of their rights should be more particularly attended to" (*Dred*, p. 297).

But Stowe shows the ultimate inefficacy of such benevolent paternalism, as Clayton wins the first trial but loses on appeal, in a scenario rendered all the more dramatic by having his father serving as the presiding judge. In Edward's reaction to the patently unjust (if technically defensible) decision, Stowe highlights the inability of even *good* southerners to escape the corruption of slavery.

Resigning his rights to practice law "in a slave state," Edward declares that his previous "hope that [slavery] might be considered a guardian institution, by which a stronger race might assume the care and instruction of the weaker one," has been unmasked as an "illusion" (*Dred*, p. 355).

Two other major legal dilemmas in the novel involve Harry and Cora Gordon, the half-siblings of Nina and Tom. These cases, even more high-stakes than Milly's, push Edward Clayton toward increasingly determined opposition against slavery, presumably bringing Stowe's readers along with him. At Nina's death, Harry was anticipating being freed based on a contract drawn up earlier to ensure that he could buy his freedom in that case. However, as the obsequious Mr Jekyl insists to Harry and Edward Clayton: "All the signatures in the world couldn't make it a valid contract," since "a slave, not being a person in the eye of the law, cannot have a contract made with him." Distraught at first but then riled to righteous anger by the threats Tom Gordon pours forth upon arrival to claim Canema (as well as Harry and Lisette) after Nina's demise, Harry boldly flees the plantation with Lisette, choosing to join Dred's band in the "dismal swamp" of the book's title rather than to remain under Tom's "Sodom and Gomorrah" brand of so-called "management on this plantation." Stunned by the confrontation between Tom and Harry, which had culminated in Harry's striking Tom before escaping, Clayton pledges to actively fight slavery (*Dred*, pp. 385, 387, 391).

We should recognize that Clayton has taken on a role similar to George Shelby's in *Uncle Tom's Cabin* – one condemning slavery's cruelty yet still hopeful about the power of one single man (especially a white man) to have a transformative influence on southern society through the force of example. Stowe mounts an even more determined critique of *slavery's power*, however, insisting that Clayton "did not know that he was already a marked man" – that those committed to maintaining the institution would now be pursuing him as one of its stalwart opponents. Clayton seeks to enlist his father's support in a reform campaign to provide slaves with legal "protection in the family state" and for "obtaining redress for injuries" (as in Milly's and Harry's cases); but Stowe's depiction of the senior Judge Clayton's worldly wise response emphasizes the impossibility of Edward's goals. Whereas Edward's mother sees some hope in his plan to gather support from southern ministers, Judge Clayton predicts that such an effort is bound to end "in Edward's expulsion from the state" (*Dred*, pp. 392–5).

When Edward does try to rouse local ministers' sense of Christian commitment, his father's prediction turns out to be more accurate than his mother's. Though not literally run off, Edward is forced to recognize how fully the southern church has been perverted by slavery. At this point, Edward's previously naïve sense of mission shifts to a more pragmatic stance, as evidenced by his response to a written plea from Harry Gordon that Clayton try to save Harry's sister Cora Gordon and her children. Clayton tries to buy Cora from Tom so as to save her. However, once again, Stowe's noble southerner can have little effect on the sickened culture of slavery: by the time he receives Harry's plea, Cora has already murdered her children rather than see them sold off as slaves, and she is therefore condemned to die by the same legal system that had previously failed to exercise justice for Milly and Harry.

By now, Edward Clayton has lost all faith in white courts and religious institutions. With this piling-on of horrors, Stowe has also prepared her readers to accept the proposition that the alternative community led by Dred for a band hidden in "the fastness of the Dismal Swamp" is actually superior to the society controlled by southern whites. Along those lines, Stowe sets forth the commitment of one upright minister (Father Dickson) to ban slaveholders from church participation, only to have him viciously attacked by Tom Gordon's vigilantes. Though she pulls back in the end from the rebellion that Dred and his followers had been planning, Stowe has established the righteousness of such revolt. In that vein, she has Dred and Harry Gordon rescue Edward Clayton from yet another of Tom's vicious assaults, then carry Edward off to the safety of Dred's "stronghold of Engedi," which Stowe clearly casts as a Biblical site of recovery and regeneration (*Dred*, pp. 494–5).

Stowe is a realistic enough chronicler of the mid-1850s south to know that such a utopian community would hardly remain secure. Accordingly, Dred himself is dead at the close of the novel, killed by Tom Gordon's fiends while trying to save another brave black, the former slave Jim. But Dred lives long enough to tell his story to his followers, and his martyrdom is far different from Tom's in Stowe's earlier anti-slavery novel. Although she follows the pattern from *Uncle Tom's Cabin* by having her young white hero (in this case, Clayton) leading former slaves with paternalistic benevolence, she reworks her disposition of the black survivors from the earlier novel, since this time those who escape the south do not emigrate to Africa, but instead settle productively within North America, some in New York and some in Canada. Overall, Stowe's second anti-slavery novel moves well beyond calling for sentimental responses to slavery on an personal level to a call for systemic reform of society. As long as slavery – with the legal, political, and religious structures supporting it – reigns in the south, this more radical novel shows, the region can never be saved. Far more forcefully than *Uncle Tom's Cabin*, therefore, Stowe's *Dred* anticipates and even implicitly justifies the violence of the Civil War.

The intensity of *Dred*'s critique of southern culture was, in fact, clearly apparent to readers of Stowe's own day, particularly in England, where the novel spawned numerous dramatizations. British stage adaptations tended both to condemn US slavery and to affirm violence as a potentially necessary tool to be used against it. Judie Newman has identified at least seventeen British dramatic versions of the story, versus fewer than half a dozen American ones, though she points out that the *Dred* plays drew reliably large audiences on both sides of the Atlantic.[38] American audiences (and thus the plays' producers) were not as ready to embrace the call to slave insurrection foregrounded in multiple British versions (with H. J. Conway's at Barnum's US theater emphasizing education and gradualism over revolt, for instance). They were also more inclined to favor comedy. Productions in the US thus expanded the roles of such minor figures from the novel as Tomtit and Tiff, who were more readily cast in minstrel mode than Dred himself.

One reason behind the relatively limited attention paid to *Dred* by American scholars has to do with the novel's being out of print for many years, but there is a chicken/egg phenomenon at work here. As a forceful leader ready to embrace violence, Dred presented a vision of black male agency that was far more difficult to manage than Tom's Christian passivity. White middle-class families could hardly be expected to purchase Dred mementos; the white-led publishing industry had little cause to render this character's story into didactic abridgements for juvenile readers or songs for parlor parties. By virtually erasing Dred (and *Dred*) from cultural memory for so many years, white America may have made it easier to overcome regional divisions in the decades since the 1860s, but this move also had the result of skewing cultural views of Harriet Beecher Stowe and her evolving views on slavery and black agency. Fortunately, recent work on this novel is showing that, even as she retained attitudes of racial essentialism so prevalent during her lifetime, Stowe at least did progress in her thinking to a point beyond *Uncle Tom's Cabin*. Accordingly, Lawrence Buell has argued that *Dred* represents "a much more significant achievement in its own right than has been recognized until very recently," and Buell himself praises the novel's starkly realistic assessment of the nation's failure to resolve the slavery issue before the Civil War.[39]

In Stowe's own day, *Dred* certainly had its fans, including the British social activist Harriet Martineau, who wrote to Stowe:

> Oh! The delight I have had in "Dred"! The genius carries all before it, and drowns everything in glorious pleasure. So marked a work of genius claims exemption from every sort of comparison; but, *as you ask for my opinion of the book*, you may like to know that I think it far superior to "Uncle Tom" . . . It seemed to me . . . that our English fiction writers had better shut up altogether and have done with it, for one will have no

patience with any but didactic writing after yours . . . I see no limit to the good it may do by suddenly splitting open Southern life, for everybody to look into. It is precisely the thing that is most wanted, – just as "Uncle Tom" was wanted three years since, to show what negro slavery in your republic was like.   (Qtd in Fields, *Life and Letters*, pp. 233–4)

The Christian Slave

Soon after making the shift from periodical serial to bound book, Stowe's first novel took to the nineteenth-century stage. Based on box office reports, we can easily speculate that many people who had never read the novel saw the play, forging their understanding of Uncle Tom and his story based solely on performance text. Consistent with genteel culture's concerns about theater's potentially corrupting influence, Stowe herself avoided the dramatizations of *Uncle Tom's Cabin* initially. She could not stop their near-immediate flourishing, however, given the joint popularity of her novel, in particular, and stage performance, in general, during the 1850s.

Despite the fact that would-be playwrights had no legal requirement in Stowe's day to involve her in productions based upon her novel, she had the opportunity to become a creative partner in staging the text early on. Soon after her serial appeared in novel form, and after unauthorized dramatizations were already cropping up, Stowe was contacted by Asa Hutchinson with a proposal for adaptation. Hutchinson, a well-known temperance singer, might have seemed the perfect choice to collaborate with Stowe. However, at that point, she was reluctant to re-envision what was still, in her mind at least, a religious text aimed at genteel Christians as a commercial product seeking a mass audience. Writing Hutchinson, she explained her misgivings in terms underscoring the view many middle-class matrons would have had toward drama in the early 1850s: "If the barrier which now keeps young people of Christian families from theatrical entertainments is once broken down by the introduction of respectable and moral plays, they will then be open to all the temptations of those who [sic] are not such, as there will be, as the world now is, five bad plays to one good."[40]

In refusing Hutchinson's offer, Stowe also cautioned him against trying to proceed alone, since the idea would be "dangerous" as "an experiment." Stowe felt the theater was too worldly a cultural site to be reformed by one story, however uplifting. Hutchinson accepted her advice. But others were already organizing productions of their own, without her involvement.

Stowe maintained a distance from those enterprises at first. But before too long she came to terms with their cultural power – not simply their appeal to what had been American theater's main audience, the working classes who packed the minstrel shows, but also their ability to draw new, middle-class audiences to *Uncle Tom's Cabin*, and thus to the anti-slavery cause. Having seen how dramatizations of her story were also reshaping perceptions of theater's place in American society, Stowe attended at least a few performances of *Uncle Tom's Cabin* herself, in one case being escorted by the socially prominent Francis H. Underwood, a co-founder of the prestigious *Atlantic Monthly* and thus a cultural arbiter whose mere presence would have sanctioned her going. Underwood reported later that Stowe clearly enjoyed seeing her novel staged: "I never saw such delight upon a human face as she displayed when she first comprehended the full power of [the actress] Mrs. Howard's *Topsy*. She scarcely spoke during the evening; but her expression was eloquent – smiles and tears succeeding each other through the whole."[41]

By the middle of the 1850s, Stowe was ready to move beyond attending a production of *Uncle Tom's Cabin* to writing her own script. Her decision to prepare that text for a single reader rather than a full staging with multiple actors is telling, however, as is her choice of performer: an African American woman, Mary Webb, wife of black writer Frank Webb. In crafting a script for only one reader, Stowe avoided the excesses which had come to be associated with some stagings of her story, such as elaborate song-and-dance production numbers and even the comic casting of "doubles" for major roles (e.g., two Toms, Topsys). Furthermore, in choosing Mary Webb, Stowe sent other important signals about her evolving views on cultural agency linked to her text, including moving away from whites' depiction of slaves in blackface and, at the same time, affirming a woman's guiding voice as the rightful avenue into the story's moral meaning.

Stowe created *The Christian Slave* with Mary E. Webb specifically in mind. Webb gave her one-woman performances of Stowe's text in both Britain and the United States throughout the 1850s. Probably the most famous of these was at Stafford House in Britain in July of 1856, when Stowe arranged for Webb to perform for an audience that included the Duchess of Sutherland and other English aristocrats well known for their involvement in the anti-slavery cause, and for their patronage of Stowe's authorship. Over time, Webb herself became closely identified with the work. A *National Anti-slavery Standard* obituary honoring Mary Webb at the time of her 1859 death directly linked her career with regular "readings of passages from 'Uncle Tom's Cabin.' "[42] Besides the pivotal occasion at Stafford House, Webb was known for performances in Philadelphia, Boston, and New York City in the US, as well as for drawing packed houses on a tour of England.

The nuances of how Webb navigated the potentially contradictory expectations various audiences would have brought to her performances are difficult to recapture, because she presented *The Christian Slave* in many venues over a number of years. Sarah Meer has identified reviews suggesting that the combination of Stowe's script and Webb's presence may have resisted the comic exaggerations that had already been linked to *Uncle Tom's Cabin* through its elaborate stagings with larger casts drawing on minstrelsy's conventions. At the same time, however, Meer feels that Stowe's script de-emphasizes female social power by reducing Eliza's role and eliminating both Mrs. Bird and Rachel Halliday. Furthermore, at least in the case of the Stafford House performance, Webb ran the risk of being perceived as an exotic commodity placed on display. Nonetheless, Mary Webb's strong presence apparently conveyed a remarkable sense of feminine self-confidence. Though the playscript includes stage directions, Webb's one-woman performances were readings. In other words, she carried the show forward alone. She stood at a lectern and used her voice as her major tool for engaging the audience. In England, reviewers were struck by her refined feminine qualities, with papers like the *Herald* and the *Daily News* invoking terms such as "mulatto lady" and "delicate" to describe her (Meer, *Uncle Tom Mania*, 187–9).

Overall, these performative occasions might be viewed as strategically echoing the way in which many members of Stowe's first audience would have encountered her narrative – having it read to them by a well-trained womanly voice in a refined, domesticated setting – but revising that scenario to empower a *black* feminine interpreter. Coming on the heels of Stowe's *Key* and before publication of *Dred, The Christian Slave* points to transitions in the author's own thinking about race issues that had been raised by some of her original readers. Along those lines, unlike the virtually countless other dramatic productions based (if often very loosely) on *Uncle Tom's Cabin, The Christian Slave* dropped some of the elements in the novel that had elicited criticism from prominent African Americans, such as the colonization-affirming transfers of Topsy and the Harris family to Liberia. Furthermore, unlike other stage adaptations, *The Christian Slave* highlighted the agency of Cassy, a figure who often disappeared entirely from other productions of the story. Thus, though notable features in the dramatic script reaffirm Stowe's sentimental racialism – by positioning George Shelby as a more forceful agent than George Harris, for instance, and by maintaining some traits of the book's minstrelsy – *The Christian Slave*'s foregrounding of Cassy is noteworthy. While a primary impetus behind this shift was surely related to Mrs Webb's being the performer, Stowe's emphasis on Cassy presented a different vision of black female agency than the other stagings of *Uncle Tom's Cabin* in the nineteenth century. Indeed, Cassy's heightened role in the drama helped lay the groundwork for a whole cluster of forceful black female characters in *Dred*, including Harry Gordon's wife Lisette and his sister Cora Gordon, as well as Milly.

Stowe's casting of Webb as the one-woman presenter for *The Christian Slave* may seem quite altruistic, indicating a wish to ensure that American blacks profited directly from the continued appeal of *Uncle Tom's Cabin*. In fact, the English tour of *The Christian Slave* supported the Webbs while Mary's husband Frank was working on his novel, *The Garies and Their Friends*. But Stowe profited as well. Her publisher regularly arranged for copies of the playscript to be sold at Webb's readings, so that audiences following along in their copies during the readings were reminded that the performance was based on Stowe's words.

Dramatizing *Uncle Tom's Cabin*

Since Stowe had no legal means to regulate the widely divergent dramatizations of *Uncle Tom's Cabin* beyond her own *Christian Slave* version, it would be inaccurate to assign her the role of author for other productions, in the traditional sense. However, over time, for audiences attending such performances, the lines between the decisions she made in originally composing *Uncle Tom's Cabin* and the reworkings of the story in others' dramatic productions blurred. Therefore, in the popular imagination, the "Tom shows" and their literary heirs became the source of most people's understanding of the characters, plot, themes, and underlying belief systems associated with the novel. Stowe's own authorial intentions and ownership were overtaken by more powerful culture-making forces, so that the "work" of *Uncle Tom's Cabin* took on a social brand of authorship beyond other literary texts.

In retrospect, the merging of American popular culture's dominant form of entertainment in the antebellum era – stage shows – and the century's best-selling novel seems a foregone conclusion. But the class divides separating the literature of social reform from public performances up until this time actually made the highly productive liaison represented by the Tom shows less than predictable. After all, the mainly male working class audiences that had filled the US minstrel halls did not read anti-slavery novels, and the proper middle-class matrons and men who first read *Uncle Tom's Cabin* in the *Era* did not typically attend stage shows. Fueling the unusual hybrid of the Tom plays was Stowe's use of minstrelsy in her novel, a move which both signaled her astute willingness to appeal to popular culture tastes and provided a connection point that antebellum producers could mine in adapting *Uncle Tom's Cabin.*

In the 1850s United States, performances based on *Uncle Tom's Cabin* faced a challenge in carving out the right mix of comic minstrelsy and tearful emotion. Blackface minstrelsy still held sway as the dominant performative genre, on the one hand, but Stowe's narrative invited new appeals to sentiment, on the other – especially in its move to position black characters as worthy of white audiences' sympathy. Antebellum dramatic adaptations of *Uncle Tom's Cabin* presented white actors in blackface playing the slaves for audiences with many members expecting that those characters would be comic, even farcical butts of race-based jokes. At the same time, at least some of those in attendance (particularly those who had read Stowe's book) would have been anticipating sentimental appeals against slavery, through calls to identify with the slave characters' suffering. Producers, writers, and actors negotiated this balancing act in a range of ways, blending minstrelsy and melodrama.

One way to document the close connections between Tom shows and minstrelsy is to note that a number of antebellum actors regularly alternated between playing roles in the plays based on Stowe's novel and performing in blackface productions, with T. D. Rice, already known as the originator of "Jim Crow," being one example. Adapting minstrel stereotypes that had depicted blacks as exaggeratedly comic or effusively sentimental, the earliest performance versions of *Uncle Tom's Cabin* represented an odd combination of anti-slavery plot and theme elements with racist characterizations linked to blackface conventions that white performers like Rice had helped establish.

While the first stagings simply pulled together pieces of the text most consistent with minstrel shows' features, what I would describe as the novel's powerful *sentimental energy* soon exerted itself over the stage versions, thereby re-shaping American theater. Before long, nineteenth-century Tom shows extended beyond brief interludes of songs and joke-filled sequences into full-fledged productions of the main storyline. The needs of drama brought some characters more to the forefront than in the book. Thus, Eliza's dramatic escape with her little child became an audience-pleasing staple; Topsy and Eva commanded ever-growing roles, due both to their inherent audience appeal and to the renown of several actresses taking on those parts. Less dramatic figures like Mrs Shelby and the Quaker Rachel Halliday disappeared. A high point of many productions was the death of little Eva, staged for the greatest possible sentimental effect. But the minstrel-oriented verbal exchanges between Miss Ophelia and Topsy – often heightened by introducing new Yankee characters to extend their jokes – also took increasing on-stage time.

Most crucially, the transfiguration of Tom from muscular and middle-aged to doting and old pandered to white audiences' discomfort with a powerful black man. In re-casting Stowe's hero, stage versions of the novel made the title character eminently appealing to white America. Abetting this transformation were such tools of the antebellum stage as nostalgic plantation songs by Stephen Foster. Foster's own career actually shifted direction through the Tom plays; his work became less oriented to the rudely comic strand of minstrelsy and more to sentimental songs like "My Old Kentucky Home" and "Old Folks at Home," frequently sung with great feeling by the actors playing Tom.

Adaptors re-told *Uncle Tom's Cabin* from a wide range of perspectives, including anti- and pro-slavery stances. A number of the plays sought a middle ground, using minstrelsy's forms to equivocate on the most radical issues raised by the novel. So, as Eric Lott has observed: "Lampooning Topsy one minute and lamenting Tom's fate the next, *Uncle Tom* was nearly as duplicitous as blackface performance – which is to say that it raised hackles on both sides of the slavery question" (Lott, *Love and Theft*, pp. 212, 218).

The antebellum productions of *Uncle Tom's Cabin* garnering the most attention from scholars have been those written by George Aiken and Henry Conway, both of which were headquartered in New York City for several months in 1853. One reason for the focus on these stagings is their intense rivalry, fueled by detailed press coverage which boosted ticket sales.

The Aiken version represented a partnership between George Aiken and George Howard, whose well-known acting family guaranteed a strong audience draw. (Little Cordelia Howard was a true star as Little Eva.) Billed as the first complete telling of *Uncle Tom's Cabin* and the most faithful to the book's anti-slavery stance, this play boasted the innovation of a full night's entertainment, in six acts. Up until this production, most stage performances in the US were a mix of variety acts, song-and-dance, jokes, tableaux-type scenes, and short skits; the practice of producing a "play" as one sequence of related scenes telling a single story was not yet popular in America. In fact, the original Aiken–Howard production dramatized only the first volume of the novel, ending with Eva's death. Its popularity quickly prompted the team to mount a second production, *The Death of Uncle Tom, or Religion of the Lowly*, based on volume two, and, soon afterwards, what was dubbed the "Grand Combination" and advertised as the "complete" *Uncle Tom's Cabin* (Williams, *Race Card*, pp. 78, 81).

Although Howard later recalled that the production manager had qualms about the plan to offer a full evening's entertainment based on the single novel, the actor himself predicted that this project would bring a new class of patrons – members of the middle classes – to the theater. With an eye toward that goal, the Aiken–Howard version emphasized themes of morality, affiliating with other reform campaigns such as temperance, and placed the angelic little Eva at the center of the story. New York's National Theater manager took the innovative step of scheduling matinées, offering the play at a time of day when middle-class patrons would more likely feel at ease in the theater's rough neighborhood.

And indeed, part of the success of the production, first in Troy, New York, and then in New York City, was its broad appeal. Ministers actually brought their congregations. On the one hand, the rough-and-tumble Bowery Boys in the pit were said to cry buckets of tears over Eliza's plight, leading reviewers to marvel at the potential shift in politics among long-time opponents of abolition, the urban working class. On the other hand, what better mark of the new respectability could Aiken's production have achieved for theaters than having Stowe herself attend one night in 1854?

Competing directly with Aiken's version was another mounted at P. T. Barnum's American Museum Theater, beginning in 1852. Known for its spectacular production elements, this show touted a Mississippi Riverboat, sending out puffs of smoke, and gorgeous panoramas of southern scenery. Barnum utilized a script created by Henry J. Conway, as originally produced in Boston. While not as explicitly pro-slavery as some other versions, particularly those produced in the south, this staging did mute the novel's critique with a happy ending allowing George Shelby to rescue Uncle Tom, converting Ophelia into a purely comic Aunty Vermont, and eliminating the politicized mother figures of the novel (Rachel Halliday, Mrs Bird, and Mrs Shelby). Amid the satisfaction of having Legree killed off, this play's incorporation of a dead villain and a restored-to-home Tom reduced the social problems of the novel to a story of individual conflict and resolution, thereby blunting Stowe's issue-oriented argument.

Just as there would be anti-Tom novels, defending slavery, so too anti-Tom plays offered counter-versions to the productions that seemed to be winning sympathy for the anti-slavery cause. Christy and Wood's Minstrels, for instance, mounted a burlesque Uncle Tom in 1854, Frank Brower created a popular "Happy Uncle Tom," and Christy's Minstrels re-framed the burlesque part of their blackface show into a "Life Among the Happy" parody. In addition, and despite the reviews describing Bowery Boys sobbing during Aiken's shows at Purdy's National Theater, there were also parodies of Uncle Tom's story aimed at Irish-American audiences (Lott, *Love and Theft*, pp. 228–9).

Pro-slavery stagings of *Uncle Tom's Cabin* used minstrelsy features to undermine the novel's original message. Plot-wise, new scenes portrayed unsuspecting blacks being carted off to the north by meddlesome (or even wicked) abolitionists. Happy songs and dances imported from minstrel shows portrayed enslaved life as charming and fun. Depictions of Uncle Tom himself in these productions played a major part in converting Stowe's heroic Christian, making principled decisions about his own life and brave service to others, into a compliant and weak figure – old, helpless, and comic.

Like the novel, play versions of Uncle Tom's story were highly popular in England. English stagings differed substantially from their American counterparts. More melodramatically gothic and violent, they were also more radical in their anti-slavery stance. (Of course, Tom plays in England had no need to bridge the political divide over slavery faced by producers in the US.) These versions placed less emphasis on the religious themes of the story; little Eva, for instance, was sometimes omitted, whereas in the US she became an iconic figure. Tom plays in Britain attracted their audiences in part by offering a kind of vicarious tourism of the US – sometimes including mis-representations of geography, speech patterns, and social practices that would have surprised Americans. Whereas Tom plays in America brought all classes together to view the same production, in England different stagings – with varying emphases – were developed for different social classes. Overall, the productions of *Uncle Tom's Cabin* in England were suited to the tastes of audiences there, and they contributed substantially to British conceptions of slavery, US culture, Stowe, and, of course, Uncle Tom.

Virtually as soon as movies existed, film versions of *Uncle Tom's Cabin* appeared. The early film versions owed debts to both the print editions and the Tom stage plays. On the one hand, book illustrations, often based in such stereotypes as a black man being beaten by a villain, were reanimated on film. On the other hand, the first-generation screen versions of Uncle Tom also incorporated familiar elements directly from the plays, such as Eliza's escape and Tom's interactions with Eva. Combining tried-and-true tableaux drawn from stage shows with interludes of slaves dancing, these films assumed audiences' familiarity with the material.

Early twentieth-century silent film versions, produced during an era attempting to re-imagine the "Old South," focused more on idealizing plantation life than on Stowe's original anti-slavery message. *Uncle Tom's Cabin: or Slavery Days* (1903) is typical, offering nostalgic images glorifying a lost way of life while minimizing the experiences of slavery itself. In this and other early movie adaptations, familiar symbols reinforced conceptions of plantations as inclusively home-like structures threatened by the intervention of misguided outsiders.

Over succeeding decades, Stowe's novel was repeatedly re-adapted for the screen, with versions in the 1930s and 1940s especially notable for their racist stereotypes, often cast in cartoon form.[43] One 1930s version featured the popular dancing duo of Shirley Temple and Bojangles Robinson. Most of these films have in common stripping away whatever dignity Stowe (how-ever misguided by romantic racialism) had provided to her hero, replacing it with the more simplistic and negative stereotypes associated with Uncle Tom today.

Not all the films of the early twentieth century waxed nostalgic over planta-tion life, however, and one striking exception actually called up the possibility of black vengeance. A 1914 film version was the first to cast a black actor, the seventy-two-year-old Sam Lucas, as Uncle Tom. Directed by Robert Daly, this version also featured the innovation of having Legree killed by a young male slave whom Tom had refused to whip. Earlier in the same film, Cassy held a gun herself and considered shooting Legree. Juxtaposing these script elements with stage versions that had also killed off Legree – but at the hands of the white hero George Shelby – Linda Williams interprets these shifts as dramatically working "against the Christian ethos of Stowe's original melodrama." Indeed, Williams points out, for white audiences "the spectacle of righteous black revenge [was] so deeply incendiary . . . that some prints of Daly's film omit the scene" of Legree's death (Williams, *Race Card*, pp. 91–3).

Though Daly's film was unusual for its time, more recent performance texts by black artists responding to *Uncle Tom's Cabin* have taken a comparably aggressive stance toward re-writing the novel and its cultural heritage. Both Bill T. Jones's *The Last Supper at Uncle Tom's Cabin* and Robert Alexander's *I Ain't Yo' Uncle: The New Jack Revisionist "Uncle Tom's Cabin"* seek to counter the layers of "comic-book caricature" that have built up over time around the character of Tom and that are continually reinforced by people whose only encounters with Stowe's work are at multiple removes, through such intervening filters as the film stereotypes outlined above.[44]

By describing Uncle Tom in the cast of characters as "a man with an image problem," playwright Alexander signals that the cultural reworkings associated with this overly familiar icon will be a major target of the "new jack" drama. But Stowe herself is identified as the main problem. Early on, Alexander has Tom ask his creator: "Why did you paint me like Jesus, instead of painting me like a man . . . a whole man?" Similarly, Topsy accuses the *Uncle Tom's Cabin* author of having foisted off destructive stereotypes on readers, and Stowe's response to these charges suggests that she and the whites she represents are still tainted by racism. "If I could dance like you, Topsy," this stage Stowe declares, "I would dance all the time."[45]

In this play, originally produced in the early 1990s by the San Francisco Mime Troupe and the Lorraine Hansberry Theater, the black characters claim their own social agency, vigorously critiquing Stowe along the way. Un-doing black-face traditions, some productions play all the white roles – except Stowe's – in whiteface, while others use multi-racial casting. Tom transforms himself on stage from a passive figure in line with the "Uncle" typically associated with his character into a forceful man in his prime – more like Stowe's original character than the stereotype, especially in the play's enactment of the final showdown with Legree. But this Tom goes well beyond reclaiming his strongest traits from the novel to join the other characters in a condemnation of Stowe and an assertion of their right to tell their own stories now. Tom accepts the need for his character to die as an indictment against slavery (keeping whites' abuses of blacks "in everybody's face"), but he also tells George Shelby off for arriving too late – again, and always.

Alexander's Stowe herself apologizes: "I was blind to many of your feelings. I misinterpreted, I misrepresented and distorted you! . . . My book should just be forgotten. It should be burned. I'm guilty." Yet Tom ignores her plea for forgiveness. Alexander's Tom insistently challenges the audience to take on the racist legacies of Stowe's text, as embodied in an angry Topsy, who warns: "I burned down Uncle Tom's condo with the nigger still in it. I love to hear glass break. I love to watch shit burn." Asks Tom, in a bitter echo of lines from the novel: "Any volunteers to take Topsy? Y'all think she come from nowhere? Do ya spects she just growed?" (Alexander, *I Ain't*, pp. 68–9).

This Tom, as interpreter of today's Topsy and re-interpreter of his own iconic self, is a very different reader than the Christian saint Stowe cast as studying the Bible under the tutelage of George Shelby and little Eva. The "new Jack" Tom offers a doubly damning indictment of Stowe's authorship – for her constraints on his character in the original novel, but also for the Stowe-derived representations of American blacks which have occurred since, and for which she is still responsible. In the ironic question reminding the audience that Topsy did not grow into her current scary self on her own, Robert Alexander assigns the nineteenth-century writer a share in the authorship of his play, along with significant responsibility for the social problems this version of *Uncle Tom's Cabin* brings to life on stage. So, we might say, all the various iterations of Uncle Tom and *Uncle Tom's Cabin*, coming together in this allusive drama, belong on the list of Stowe's "works," and become a part of her heritage, for good or ill.

Travel writing

Although she would never again match the impact she had achieved with *Uncle Tom's Cabin*, Stowe was a highly productive literary professional for many years afterward. Along the way, she helped shape several nineteenth-century literary genres, including travel writing.

Sunny Memories of Foreign Lands

By the late nineteenth century, well-to-do women like Jane Addams would consider taking the Grand Tour of Europe an essential ingredient in their educations, with the practice having become common enough for Henry James to satirize it in 1879's *Daisy Miller*. But in the 1850s, when Stowe made her first trip across the Atlantic, such journeys were far less commonplace for American women than they would become in succeeding decades.

Between Stowe's first journey abroad and her last, factors opening up European travel to more middle-class Americans included improved transportation systems, increased wealth, and a growing sense that Europe was a site for both personal learning and acquiring high-status consumer goods. Stowe's writing about Europe in *Sunny Memories* contributed to that trend, while helping support what Mary Suzanne Schriber has described as the feminization of travel writing. Schriber points to several recurring traits in post-bellum international travel narratives, including rhetorical moves to domesticate far-away places and to re-envision American life in light of experiences abroad.[46] As an early practitioner, Stowe, like Margaret Fuller and Catharine Maria Sedgwick, would use her European travel writing to re-define her own identity in more public terms. That effort involved engaging with longstanding questions about the relationship between the United States and Europe.

In the front matter for her first travel memoir, published in 1854, Stowe explained that her book would be "what its name denotes, 'Sunny Memories.'" Anticipating that some might fault her for excessive enthusiasm, Stowe warned,

> If there be characters and scenes that seem drawn with too bright a pencil, the reader will consider that, after all, there are many worse sins than a disposition to think and speak well of one's neighbors. To admire and to love may now and then be tolerated, as a variety, as well as to carp and criticize. America and England have heretofore abounded towards each other in illiberal criticisms.[47]

Stowe's allusion to "illiberal criticisms" referred in part to the sometimes-negative relations between the two countries, a lingering result of the Revolutionary War. While many Americans still identified with England, others were intent on developing a distinctively American culture.

Stowe's preface was also invoking the longstanding tendency of English cultural arbiters to denigrate America as a backwater. Specifically, Stowe's reference recalled the negative stance British authors – especially Frances Trollope and Charles Dickens – had adopted in writing about their American journeys. By indicating that her report of travel in the opposite direction would be willing "to admire and to love," Stowe proposed a truce. She was savvy enough to know that the British response to *Uncle Tom's Cabin* represented a career boost with potential long-term impact, one she could strengthen by celebrating England itself in *Sunny Memories*.

Even more so than Europeans, however, the audience for *Sunny Memories* was Americans of Stowe's own social class. With these readers in mind, Stowe used a device made familiar in earlier accounts by Europeans of their journeys through America – a series of travel letters. The addressee for the book's letters was an American "Aunt E," whose supposed lack of knowledge about Europe allowed the author to educate, as well as to amuse, her readers. Sometimes Stowe made fun of herself and her traveling companions as they encountered unfamiliar sights. At the same time, she maintained a friendly, almost folksy voice that helped readers envision themselves as capable of such a journey, and overseas travel itself as well worth the effort. If she could not resist including teacher-like lectures with historical and geographical data, Stowe still conveyed such unbridled enthusiasm for her topic that her book may well have encouraged increased bookings on transatlantic ships and in European hotels. Her astute rhetorical strategies effectively turned the publication into "a travel guide that tourists carried under their arms as they would later carry Baedecker's and Fodor's" (Hedrick, *HBS*, p. 266).

One of the ways that Stowe's *Sunny Memories* made Europe seem easily accessible was by reading the sights through a framework which both Americanized the exotic and insisted upon the sentimental connections linking people from different cultures. An April 1853 entry from Glasgow, Scotland, is a case in point. She predicts that "Aunt E" will "sympathize in the emotions" associated with the author's first views of Scotland, "a country whose history and literature, interesting enough of itself, has become to us still more so, because the reading and learning of it formed part of our communion for many a social hour." Scotland may be far away from New England, she admits, but it is already familiar from previous family study. Stowe asserts that the "views of Scotland" which she is now seeing in person are, in fact, the same ones "which lay on my mother's table, even while I was a little child, and in poring over which I spent so many happy, dreamy hours." Invoking Burns, Scott, and the Scottish ballads, she is also calling up the power of literature, which links her visit to European sights with her community at home: "So in coming near to Scotland, I seemed to feel not only my own individuality, but all that my friends would have felt, had they been with me" (*SM*, p. 41).

Of course, most readers of *Sunny Memories* would not actually have the same access to Europe that Stowe and her family could claim. By the second time she crossed the Atlantic, Stowe had become quite comfortable interacting with aristocrats, international politicians, and literary figures like Lady Byron,

Charles Kingsley, Lady Labouchere, and Harriet Martineau in England; Rosa Bonheur, Madame de Staël, Madame Mohl, and Madame Belloc (one of the translators of *Uncle Tom's Cabin*) in France. Stowe had also progressed from being amazed by the rather scandalous figures of artists like Rubens on her first trip to encouraging her twin daughters' growing love of opera on her second.

Agnes of Sorrento

By 1859, when Stowe took her all of her children (save Charles) along on her third trip to Europe, she was an accomplished traveler. Eager to tour Italy, she first handled her business of securing an international copyright for *The Minister's Wooing*, then headed to Florence and the picturesque towns around the Bay of Naples. Caught in Salerno by a storm, Stowe and her traveling companions spent an evening of story-telling, with Stowe generating the core idea for *Agnes of Sorrento*. The narrative appeared first as a serial, running in the *Atlantic Monthly* from May 1861 through April 1862, and in London's *Cornhill Magazine* on a parallel schedule.

Though certainly not literally a tour guide, the novel guides readers through an imaginative encounter with Italian culture. If *Sunny Memories* offered a practical introduction to Europe, *Agnes of Sorrento* took on a larger intellectual problem for Stowe and other Americans of her self-consciously Protestant social class – how to incorporate European art, history, and culture into their own world view. For Stowe, this question was crucial, since much of what she had been experiencing in her tours abroad ran counter to her upbringing, including her family's Puritan heritage, with its aversion to the arts and to Catholicism. In that vein, ever-convinced of her social class's special responsibility to educate others, Stowe sought ways to process what she was learning overseas and to re-present it to Americans back home in a useable form.

In *Agnes of Sorrento*, Stowe once again called upon the feminized ways of writing that had served her well in *Uncle Tom's Cabin*. She situated her examination of social issues within a domestic plot. Also, she emphasized concrete imagery over abstractions, creating a narrative full of pictures to present a complex argument. In this case, the pictures were not just vivid characterizations – though *Agnes of Sorrento* has these – but also literal pictures, various works of art tied to Italian Catholic culture from multiple eras. Indeed, part of what Stowe explored in the novel was how to draw upon art for cultural understanding and how to use "readings" of art for religious purposes. To access the cultural capital Italy offered for addressing these questions – important to Stowe as a writer, a Protestant Christian, and an American now fully enamored with travel – she created a story with parable-like qualities.

The introduction to *Agnes of Sorrento* for the *Atlantic* was reprinted in the book version. This prefatory piece identified two real-life Italian models for major characters – the heroine, Agnes, and her grandmother, Elsie. Though seen first as "a beautiful young girl," "sitting at an orange stand," and a "woman straight and tall, with silver hair, Roman nose, and dark eyes," the two Italian women who worked their way into Stowe's narrative should not, she says, be read in literal terms but instead as coming from a "whole golden scene [which] receded centuries back." This, Stowe explains, is how she and the members of her party interpreted the real-life counterparts for Agnes and Elsie, by seeing the two "in a vision as they might and must have been in other days." This imaginative approach to "seeing" Europe – specifically, the rich Catholic culture of Italy – is what Stowe wants to convey to her American readers, providing them vicarious access to the cultural capital her group acquired from their own visit. Indeed, to stress that her account is really about interpretation, she closes her introduction with a reference to her traveling group carrying roses away from Sorrento – fresh flowers they knew would not survive literally, but could live as "memory" and "an emblem."[48]

Set in a purposefully vague past era, *Agnes of Sorrento* follows the title character through a spiritual growing-up process. Naïve and angelic at the outset, Agnes maintains her pure heart while acquiring a more complex, informed view of religion. Having long assumed that she will enter a convent, Agnes does not know how to manage her own feelings when she finds herself attracted to the bold young cavalier, Agostino Sarelli. Her grandmother is overly protective because of Agnes's mother having been abandoned by a libertine. Her local priest, while claiming to have Agnes's interests at heart, actually feels a lustful attraction to her. But her maternal uncle, Father Antonio, is both an artist and a true priest, and he gently leads Agnes to understand how she can serve God while also becoming a wife and mother. A major turning point for Agnes comes through a pilgrimage to Rome, where she had expected to find guidance from the Holy Father but instead encountered the corruption of the Borgia papacy firsthand when kidnapped by this evil Pope's servants and barely saved in time by Agostino. As a counterpoint to Borgia sinfulness, Stowe offers a Savonarola figure foreshadowing the Protestant Martin Luther. In a broader sense, she presents a vision of religion that synthesizes Catholicism's emphasis on maternal goodness with Protestantism's corrective of the Rome-based faith's excesses.

Closely bound to this blending process is Stowe's vision of art as an avenue to religious understanding. The character of Agnes is, on one level, an art-like text other characters often misinterpret. For example, while some try to reduce her to a sexless Mary figure, others see only an object of lust. But, images like a Saint

Agnes statue that has Christianized a pagan nymph point to a different vision of Agnes – as woman and as art – understood through a both/and perspective, incorporating "at once the pagan physical idea of Woman and the Christian ideal of spiritual, virgin purity." Once Agostino comes to this inclusive reading of Agnes and what she represents – finally seeing her "as a sacrament, the combination of an earthly sign and a spiritual grace" – they can embrace a holy Christian marriage.[49]

In reading this story about how to "read" Agnes and what she might represent, Stowe's audience can learn how to interpret art, particularly texts (like this Sorrento-based story) drawn from the rich culture of Italy. By demonstrating that this foreign space can provide adaptable exempla, Stowe reassures her readers that Europe itself can be a transportable cultural text. Thus, for example, Catholicism, which elsewhere in writing by Stowe and other Beecher family members had been portrayed as an evil force, becomes now a resource to be mined, even if only selectively.[50] Female figures like Agnes and the Virgin Mary can be role models. And art itself can draw from both classical (pagan) and Catholic sources to benefit American culture.

Palmetto Leaves

"If you want to live in an orange-orchard, you must give up wanting to live surrounded by green grass."[51] So Stowe advised the readers of *Palmetto Leaves*, a collection of Florida sketches published in 1873. In 1867, Harriet and Calvin had bought a winter home near Orange Park. As in her multiple European trips, Stowe was helping inaugurate a trend by traveling back and forth between New England and the south each year. She admitted as much in "The Wrong Side," one of the *Palmetto Leaves* sketches, where she described the area around Mandarin on the St Johns River: "Florida is peculiarly adapted to the needs of people who can afford two houses and want a refuge from the drain that winter makes on health," she explained (*PL*, p. 38).

It was not, her sketches showed, a climate where she would live all year. Nor was it suitable for year-round industry. Florida, at least in Stowe's southern sketches, was a charming if somewhat quirky place of escape. Though Stowe's sketches generally depict her family living a "breezy, open-aired" and casual life in Florida (*PL*, p. 66), biographical details indicate her Mandarin winters were not entirely carefree. One impulse behind being there was to participate in the educative efforts of Reconstruction; indeed, Stowe's family helped establish a school for local black and white children. In addition, while the pace of her writing slowed down, the *Palmetto Leaves* sketches themselves make clear that she worked – even when others in her family only played. We can see from her correspondence that she often juggled multiple writing projects while in the south each year. Nonetheless, life in Florida was relatively relaxed, even for the perpetually busy Harriet Beecher Stowe. Enhanced interaction with the outdoors slowed her daily pace without sacrificing comfort considerably. After all, as in New England, she had servants. And, though her sketches describe the Stowes' Mandarin home as a "cottage," it was a large, well-appointed structure surrounded by an orange grove.

The *Palmetto* sketches themselves are uneven in quality and unstable in stance, in part because Stowe shifts back and forth between an insider and an outsider/observer perspective. Some segments (as in "Letter-Writing" and "Buying Land in Florida") present themselves as chatty, in-the-know responses to queries sent "from all States of the Union" by readers of earlier magazine pieces (*PL*, p. 175). Others contemplate the plants and animals around Stowe's Mandarin home. A few are occasional pieces, such as one account of a particular trek south, with a stop in Savannah, and another about an excursion to Saint Augustine. Several pieces read like a version of her earlier *Sunny Memories* transplanted to the southern United States. Exuding enthusiasm in "Letter to the Girls" and "A Water-Coach," for instance, Stowe offers a virtual advertisement for winter fun in Florida. Exploring the woods for flowers (available all winter, Stowe promises), bird-watching, and boat-riding are just a few of her recommended activities.

Stowe does acknowledge the less appealing dimensions of Florida. In "The Wrong Side of the Tapestry" she cautions tourists who may come with false expectations. She complains about the railroad to Saint Augustine and emphasizes how hot the summers are. She points to both the advantages and disadvantages of having the closest neighbor be five miles away: "Our neighbor over the way is not, to be sure, quite so near or so observable as if one lived on Fifth Avenue or Broadway" (*PL*, p. 225).

If Stowe's tone shifts are a bit disconcerting, her portrayals of local blacks are downright offensive. Negative stereotypes scream off the page, even in a sketch apparently crafted to gain sympathy for freedmen adjusting to their new status. In "Old Cudjo and the Angel," Stowe tells of an "aged negro, misshapen and almost deformed" whom she and her husband met on the wharf near their home. Cudjo's single bale of cotton is all that remains from a farm he had bought and worked for four years, only to be told he must vacate it when the paperwork from his purchase turns out to be flawed. The climax of the story recounts how a white neighbor has helped Cudjo reclaim his land, and Stowe's descriptions of her title character show that her essentialist view of race differences had not changed from the 1850s. To characterize Cudjo, she says: "He was black as night itself; and but for a glittering, intellectual eye, he might have been taken for a big baboon, – the missing link of Darwin" (*PL*, p. 269).

Later, in a string of reductive racist descriptions in "The Laborers of the South," Stowe similarly undercuts her stated argument that blacks can be industrious workers for rebuilding the region. For example, she posits that "the negro laborer *carefully looked after* is as good as any that can be hired at the North. In some respects they are better. As a class they are more obedient, better natured, more joyous, and easily satisfied" (*PL*, p. 315, italics in original).

When we set such descriptions of Stowe's black neighbors in Florida within the larger context of her reports from Mandarin, we can see that, like most travel writing, *Palmetto Leaves* is as much about its author as about the place it purports to categorize. We can also see that in this text, unlike in her New England novels, Stowe sometimes takes on what Marjorie Pryse has classified as a distancing "local color" rather than an affirming "regional" stance. (See discussion of New England regionalist fiction in the next section.) In line with this distancing perspective, in her final years, Stowe chose New England over Florida, first nursing her husband when his health declined and then slipping herself into a kind of mental twilight. At that point, her only travels were around her Hartford neighborhood. As her friend Annie Fields would describe these final journeys, so highly circumscribed, "She became 'like a little child,' wandering about, pleased with flowers, fresh air, the sound of a piano, or a voice singing hymns, but the busy, inspiring spirit was asleep" (Fields, *Life and Letters*, p. 392).

New England regionalist fiction

Stowe's New England novels – especially *The Pearl of Orr's Island*, *The Minister's Wooing*, and *Oldtown Folks* – are gaining increased critical attention as regionalist fiction. In an appreciative reading of "Uncle Lot"/ "A New England Sketch" alongside the later novels of New England, Marjorie Pryse has noted how these works exemplify differences between so-called "local color" writing and the very different brand of regionalist fiction Pryse and Judith Fetterley have been studying. As Pryse explains, unlike local color writing, which is "looking and laughing *at* rural, poor, and disenfranchised regional people," "literary regionalism . . . locates the social and cultural perspectives of the regional characters who live and speak in its pages in ways these characters would recognize as their own, and it does so without holding them up to ridicule or allowing them to serve as yardsticks of the queer which then enable readers outside the place or from urban centers to assert the measure of their own normality."[52]

Stowe's New England novels certainly fit Pryse's definition. In doing so, they embody a trend historian Joseph A. Conforti has described as crucial to the sustained process of "imagining" New England into a "national regionalism," with the communities Stowe depicts in these novels being stand-ins for the nation as a whole. From Conforti's perspective, Stowe was an influential player in this process, as her work "repeatedly returned to the same village landscape" and imbued it with "a moral standing" appealing especially to "the scores of transplanted Yankees in New York and the West."[53]

The Pearl of Orr's Island

Stowe started *The Pearl of Orr's Island* in 1852, but it would be ten years before she finished it. Initially, the need to respond to criticism of *Uncle Tom's Cabin* diverted her energies to her *Key*; then her first European trip intervened; then the events of "bleeding Kansas" turned her attention to *Dred*. After her third journey overseas, Stowe did go back to *The Pearl*, only to be sidetracked again by the opportunity to develop *Agnes of Sorrento* (which she had begun in Italy) into a serial. Stowe had optimistically thought that she could manage two novels simultaneously – her Maine story, which she had begun printing in the *Independent*, and the new Italian one. In 1861, partway through both narratives, she halted work on *The Pearl of Orr's Island* again so as to finish *Agnes of Sorrento* first.[54] Although she did complete *The Pearl*, she was not able to resolve tensions between the critique of gender roles around her major characters, with which she began, and the celebration of regional strengths, seen mainly in appealing minor characters.

The first half of the novel focuses on the education of two children, Mara and Moses, both of whom are orphaned in the early pages. Mara is born in a moment of tragedy, just after her mother has seen her father's incoming ship sink. With her mother having succumbed to shock and grief, Mara is raised by her grandparents, the Pennels, who also adopt Moses when he washes up on land after another shipwreck. Though their shared upbringing makes them close, Stowe emphasizes from the outset that her two main characters have contrasting natures, partly based in gender. Mara is allowed to share in Moses's early educational training, but she does not have access to the wider opportunities that await him beyond their village. Significantly, while he is at sea, she matures beyond him intellectually and spiritually, in large part under the enlightened moral tutelage of the Toothacre sisters and Captain Kittridge. Mara develops such a strong reflective spirituality that Moses, having returned to the village, hardly seems worthy of her, despite his professed love. So Stowe consigns her heroine to a sentimental death. As Mara's health declines, Moses is finally truly attentive to her, acquiring spiritual strength from their final days together. Much later, Moses marries Sally, a formerly flirtatious but now good-hearted friend who, like Moses, has been reformed through Mara's love.

Some critics have suggested that Stowe's stop-and-restart approach to writing the book led to a disjointed narrative for *The Pearl*. But the novel has found defenders, including Gillian Brown, Marjorie Pryse, and Judith Fetterley, all of whom see thematic strengths in the text. Brown praises Stowe's creative approach to depicting a "conversion narrative," wherein Mara's study of both written and oral texts (including Captain Kittridge's tales) leads her to develop an appreciation for spiritual over earthly values. Pryse dubs *The Pearl* "one of Stowe's most significant accomplishments," especially for "portraying the complexity of regional characters." For Pryse, figures like Captain Kittridge and the two village aunts, Roxy and Ruey Toothacre, are models of regionalist writing, helping the main character Mara achieve an appealing "mother-centered spirituality." Similarly, Fetterley praises the novel's rejection of the courtship plot that would have ended with Mara and Moses together. In its stead, Fetterley points out, Stowe's novel shows the eventual uplift of Moses through a feminized spiritual curriculum potentially more powerful than either masculine alternative he had tried – book-learning with the local Reverend Sewell or manly adventures at sea. *The Pearl of Orr's Island* – Mara herself – turns out to be the richest source of knowledge and spiritual love. If the novel winds up sacrificing Mara so as to save Moses, it also tears the hero's excessively aggressive (and masculine) world view down so as to lift him up, eventually, into a new humility. In Fetterley's view, therefore, the narrative may have been difficult to write in part because of the challenging ideas – especially around gender relations – Stowe was trying to confront, so that this work surely deserves attention for its unresolved complexity.[55]

The Minister's Wooing, Oldtown Folks, and Poganuc People

Stowe set three of her New England novels in various decades after the American Revolution, in different villages with parallel social structures. In all of these narratives, she highlighted shortcomings associated with Calvinist ideology while showing that the culture of her ancestors did still have valuable legacies to offer nineteenth-century America.

The Minister's Wooing, set in Newport, Rhode Island, was first published in 1859. Stowe's heroine, Mary Scudder, lives with her widowed mother and their boarder, the local minister, Dr Hopkins. Stowe modeled the minister on Samuel Hopkins, an historical figure known for his early opposition to slavery (which Stowe celebrates) and his adherence to the viewpoints of Jonathan

Edwards (which the author questions). As hinted in the title, the stern yet caring Hopkins becomes a suitor for Mary's hand, but he has two rivals – young James Marvyn and another historical character, Aaron Burr.

In Stowe's view, neither Hopkins nor Burr is a suitable choice for Mary. Hopkins earns her respect through such enlightened work as persuading the Marvyns to free their slave, Candace, and delivering a stirring anti-slavery sermon. But Hopkins exhibits Edwardsean religion's flaws as well as its strengths: when James Marvyn seems to have died at sea, the minister echoes Lyman Beecher's response to Catharine's loss of her fiancé years earlier by insisting that, having shown no clear conviction of his own salvation, Marvyn must not have been elected for heaven. (The tragic drowning of Stowe's son Henry may have helped inspire this plot element.) Burr, like Hopkins, has ties to Jonathan Edwards, from whom the Revolutionary hero has descended. But Burr is wayward and worldly. Thus, if Hopkins is too sternly Calvinist a choice for Mary, Burr is the flip side – a man not spiritual enough.

With Mary representing the nation, we see that Stowe is advising her country to draw on the best strengths of her regional heritage while rejecting its flaws. When James Marvyn returns, Hopkins does (eventually) show the kindness at the heart of his Calvinism by releasing Mary from her betrothal, which had occurred after she believed her first love to be dead. In the meantime, though, Stowe forcefully posits her view of Candace, Mary, and Mrs. Marvyn as alternative spiritual leaders for the community – and, by extension, for America – through the loving, feminized theology they envision together in response to James's apparent death. Thus, in the personal stories of her characters, Stowe offers what Susan K. Harris has called "a moral, intellectual, and affective history for New England" that also provides a program for pre-Civil War America to follow: freeing its slaves and embracing women-centered spiritual values while honoring its Revolutionary past.[56]

Drawn in part from Calvin Stowe's memories of his youth in Massachusetts, *Oldtown Folks* was published ten years after *The Minister's Wooing*, though it was set in the same 1790s timeframe. If for the earlier novel Stowe was still caught up in the antebellum slavery issue, by the time she wrote *Oldtown Folks*, the political landscape had shifted. In this case a key concern is to recover the optimistic spirit and unity of the era just after the Revolution, now that the nation is attempting to manage post-Civil War Reconstruction. Again, as in her previous regionalist fiction, Stowe suggests that the answers to the nation's contemporary dilemmas may be found in examining the past to construct a blend of history and myth.

Stowe herself hoped that *Oldtown Folks* would be her literary masterpiece, but the novel met with a mixed reception. Dorothy Berkson says the book offers a "rich tapestry of New England customs and characters" and "provides remarkable insights into the complex connections between politics and religion."[57] However, as Bret Harte suggested in Stowe's own day, readers might well have had difficulty seeing relevant links between the country's post-Civil-War situation and the Calvinist theological debates Stowe highlighted in this book. Harte himself judged that Stowe's insistent looks back to figures like Jonathan Edwards and John Winthrop had "as little to do with the present civilization as the aborigines."[58] Another point of criticism has been Stowe's choice of narrator, the rather plodding Horace Holyoke (modeled on young Calvin Stowe). Whatever the novel's faults, Stowe did create some memorable regionalist characters, particularly the folksy commentator Sam Lawson (whom she would re-activate in *Oldtown Fireside Stories*) and the womanly local leaders, Miss Mehitable Rossiter and Grandmother Badger. Furthermore, if Horace is unexciting, he is at least surrounded by a constellation of interesting friends – Harry Percival, Esther Avery (probably modeled on Stowe), and Tina Percival – not to mention Ellery Davenport, a reconfiguration of the scoundrel-like Aaron Burr from *The Minister's Wooing*.

By the time she turned to *Poganuc People* in the late 1870s, when she was almost seventy years old, Stowe had grown tired of the New England village genre herself. A letter to her son Charles declared: "I would much rather have written another such book as 'Footsteps of the Master' [a series of religious meditations], but all, even the religious papers, are gone mad on serials. Serials they demand and will have, and I thought, since this generation will listen to nothing but stories, why not tell them?" When she sent the manuscript of *Poganuc People* off to Oliver Wendall Holmes and his wife, Stowe enclosed a letter identifying them as "being among the few who know" about those earlier times and said of her last novel: "It is an extremely quiet story for these sensational days, when heaven and earth seem to be racked for a thrill; but as I get old[,] I do love to think of those quiet, simple times when there was not a poor person in the parish, and the changing glories of the year were the only spectacle" (qtd in Fields, *Life and Letters*, p. 373).

Her complaint to son Charles aside, Stowe infused this last novel with a religious spirit and related nostalgia, as expressed to her friend and editor-colleague Holmes. Dolly, the major character, is the daughter of a minister, and she reenacts many of the author's youthful experiences. Younger than most of her siblings, Dolly strikes up cross-generational and cross-class friendships to avoid loneliness. These connections turn out to be a boon, opening up the deeper dimensions of village life to Dolly, even at an early age.

Through Dolly, *Poganuc People* addresses a number of Stowe's abiding questions about religion's place in American life. Dolly's father the Reverend

Cushing is a Congregationalist, but many in the community are joining the new Episcopal church, which was Stowe's own eventual affiliation. This division of the village raises practical questions, such as how best to celebrate Christmas. The broader challenge is how to create unity in a place no longer united under one Church. Stowe stresses how a cross-denominational revival led by Dr. Cushing and the July celebration of US Independence Day reunite everyone in the village, suggesting that shared Christian religious commitment can still be central to American culture, despite denominational differences. Writing around the time of the nation's centennial, she envisions a strong moral spirit to support national unity.

Additional late-career writings

Along with her ongoing fascination with New England regional culture, Stowe's oeuvre exhibits other sustained commitments, including writing about religion, household management, and social issues around gender. Stowe's comment to her son that she would like to have written more books like her *Footsteps of the Master* project indicates how important spirituality was becoming to her at that point in her life. A sequence of devotional texts geared to the calendar of holy days, *Footsteps* (1877) was Stowe's most explicitly ministerial of books, but it was hardly her only religious one. When the Riverside Press assembled the commemorative set of Stowe's works soon after her death, one entire volume was devoted to religious writing, with numerous sketches and poems complementing a re-printing of *Footsteps*. Some of these pieces had initially appeared as far back as the 1830s, showing that religion had always been central to her authorship.

Topics on home life also held her interest from her earliest family letters to one of her final publications, in 1880, when she playfully presented a collection of domestic stories for children called *A Dog's Mission; or, the Story of the Old Avery House*. In between, her works on moral domestic management included numerous magazine stories for children and parents to read together. In the mid-1860s, *House and Home Papers* and *The Little Foxes* drew from Stowe's *Atlantic* domestic sketches, under the name Christopher Crowfield, and blended satirical pieces like "The Ravages of a Carpet" with more straightforwardly moral discussions between Crowfield and his family members, as in "Home Religion." Stowe's popular domestic essays for the *Atlantic* audience during this period have been linked with then-editor James Fields's recognition of women readers' importance to the magazine and have even been said to explain why the periodical's main competitor, *Harper's*, inaugurated a domestic department.[59] In 1869, J. B. Ford and Company published *The

American Woman's Home, one of the century's most influential domestic advice books. Updating Catharine Beecher's 1841 *Treatise on Domestic Economy* by adding sketches from Stowe, the collaborative project stressed the inextricable links between effective home management and Christian morality. Around the same time (1868–9), Stowe was working as a co-editor and major contributor for *Hearth and Home* magazine, where she interwove housekeeping advice with more politicized editorializing (such as pro-suffrage statements) and suggestions to would-be women writers.[60]

At the center of all Stowe's writing on the home – in non-fiction as well as fiction – is a commitment to a woman's work there. Whether laying out ideal organizational plans for the middle-class kitchen in an advice text or extolling a fireside as the center of domestic and political life for a fictional New England village, Stowe celebrates women's capacity to lead.

Slavery was the social issue that produced *Uncle Tom's Cabin*, Stowe's most famous literary work, and formal celebrations of her career near the end of her life cast her anti-slavery contributions as her major legacy. However, when surveying all her writing, we see that gender, even more than race, most consistently held Stowe's attention as a subject and as an interpretive lens for doing cultural work. One place where this abiding interest is clear is in the gender-based social critique from the 1870s, including her defense of Lady Byron and several novels.

During her second 1850s trip to England, Stowe had met privately with Lady Byron, who outlined details of the Byrons' painful marriage. These stories must have been upsetting to Stowe, who, like so many others of her generation, had idolized the dashing, famous poet in her youth. When Lady Byron sought advice on how to respond to the gossip about her marriage's collapse, Stowe recommended that her friend remain silent. Later, after Lady Byron's death, a book by Byron's mistress (Countess Guiccioli) painted a highly negative portrait of his wife while continuing to feed the myth of the poet's misunderstood romantic identity. Stowe felt compelled to respond with an 1869 *Atlantic* essay, "The True Story of Lady Byron's Life."

Stowe's account revealed what Lady Byron had confided back in 1856 – that Byron had an incestuous relationship with his sister, Augusta Leigh, resulting in a daughter; that he had tried to force his wife to acquiesce to a continuation of the affair; that he had been abusive during much of their time together; and that, rather than her abandoning him, Byron had forced her from their home. Stowe turned Byron's own poetry against him, quoting long passages of several works as support for her charges.

Stowe's version of Lady Byron's story emphasizes her friend's saintly patience and attributes her long silence about her husband to feminine deference. Stowe also counters portrayals of Lady Byron as a cold-hearted monster by cataloguing ways in which the abandoned wife gave herself over to benevolent projects, including sponsoring schools for the poor and supporting the fugitive slaves William and Ellen Craft. Portraying Byron himself as alternating between helpless insanity and reckless cruelty, Stowe insists that, after the marriage breakdown, Lady Byron patiently assumed a maternal stance toward her estranged spouse: "Through all this sorrowful history was to be seen, not the care of a slandered woman to make her story good, but the pathetic anxiety of a mother who treasures every particle of hope, every intimation of good, in the son whom she cannot cease to love."[61]

The reaction to Stowe's essay was immediate and punitive. Both Stowe's family and the *Atlantic* took a financial hit, to the extent that some have blamed the sale of Oakholm, Stowe's elaborate home in Nook Farm, as well as declining *Atlantic* subscriptions, on the story's aftermath. Her fan base in England evaporated. Stowe had a few defenders, including her neighbor Mark Twain, who wrote a column for the *Buffalo Express* to defend Lady Byron's defender. Elizabeth Cady Stanton and Susan B. Anthony, hoping Stowe's Byron piece augured well for her becoming more active in the suffrage movement, also rallied to her aid. Stirred up even more by the vituperative attacks, Stowe extended the controversy by writing the book-length *Lady Byron Vindicated* (1870), calling upon her women's rights activist sister Isabella Beecher Hooker for assistance in preparing the manuscript.

This collaboration with Isabella was unusual. The two sisters would later be on opposite sides during the scandal over their brother Henry Ward Beecher's alleged affair with a parishioner, when Harriet supported Henry and Isabella believed his accusers. Overall, Isabella was far more radical in her positions on women's rights and more aggressively involved in the movement's politics. In the case of the Byron battle, however, the two sisters were of one mind. While Stowe framed her argument for the book in personal terms, she built on previous experience confronting legal injustice in *A Key to Uncle Tom's Cabin* and *Dred* to offer at least an implicit call for reform. Thus, "More than an anecdotal defense of Lady Byron from charges that she had failed her wifely obligations, Stowe's text is a defense of women's rights and an argument for gender equality in marriage."[62]

Stowe is sometimes critiqued today for failing to lend more weight to causes like suffrage, a movement she occasionally praised (as in writing for *Hearth and Home*) but for which she would not become a public organizer. Perhaps because of the brutal response to her writing on Lady Byron, perhaps because of her ingrained sense of female deference, Stowe refrained from taking radical stands on any women's issues in the social satire novels she wrote during the 1870s, such as *Pink and White Tyranny* (1871), *My Wife and I* (1872), and *We and Our Neighbors* (1875). As Carolyn Karcher observes, these fictional works share a commitment to protest which is also evident in non-fiction pieces like *A Key to Uncle Tom's Cabin* and *Lady Byron Vindicated.*[63] Specifically, they share an impulse to critique the social construction of gender roles – thereby marking Stowe as ahead of her time – while also insisting that women cannot (yet) overcome those constraints – thereby showing that she could not envision a full-scale revolt.

In *Pink and White Tyranny*, for instance, Stowe warns her readers that her narrative is less a novel than "a parable," and that she aims to present a "moral."[64] In describing her central character, a Lillie anticipating Edith Wharton's Lily Bart, Stowe insists that the flaws sure to cause John Seymour great pain in their marriage are not so much Lillie's fault as society's:

> Pretty girls, unless they have wise mothers, are more educated by the opposite sex than by their own. Put them where you will, there is always some man busying himself in their instruction; and the burden of masculine teaching is generally about the same, and might be stereotyped as follows: "You don't need to be or do any thing. Your business in life is to look pretty, and amuse us. You don't need to study: you know all by nature that a woman need to know."   (*PWT*, p. 47)

Though Stowe's satire through much of the novel calls for un-doing socialization processes warping American women, she closes the narrative with a conservative argument about marriage:

> It has been very surprising to us to see in these our times that some people, who really at heart have the interest of women upon their minds, have been so short-sighted and reckless as to clamor for an easy dissolution of the marriage-contract, as a means of righting their wrongs. Is it possible that they do not see that this is a liberty which, once granted, would always tell against the weaker sex? If the woman who finds that she has made a mistake, and married a man unkind or uncongenial, may, on the discovery of it, leave him and seek her fortune with another, so also may a man.   (*PWT*, p. 319)

Even in the 1870s, Stowe faced some criticism for failing to take as determined a stand on women's issues as she had done on slavery in the 1850s. Yet, her approach to social protest was consistent throughout her career. She was more intent on highlighting problems than on laying out a detailed plan for solving them, more inclined to try converting individuals' feelings toward enlightened perspectives than she was to take on a political process of reform herself.

At the turn into the twentieth century, her strategy was still seen as relevant by other writers eager to address social issues. When Upton Sinclair published

The Jungle in 1906, just ten years after her death and a little over half a century since the original serialization of Stowe's anti-slavery bestseller, he purposefully affiliated his novel with *Uncle Tom's Cabin*, identifying his subject as "the life of the modern slave – the slave of the factory, the sweatshop, and the mine," and hoping that his text might rally support to this cause as effectively as her work had done for southern chattel slavery decades earlier.[65] Commentators ranging from Eugene Debs to Jack London responded to the cue, using language from Stowe to authorize Sinclair's writing, with London declaring: "Here it is at last! What 'Uncle Tom's Cabin' did for black slaves, 'The Jungle' has a large chance to do for the white slaves of today."[66] One hundred years later, Stowe has become a less desirable model. When Scott Turow was asked if his *Reversible Errors* novel could be "the *Uncle Tom's Cabin* of capital punishment," the author of a string of popular legal dramas exclaimed: "That's exactly what I don't want to do!," since he "believe[s] in the old saying, 'If you want to send a message, use Western Union.' "[67]

Stowe's whole writing career was, indeed, about sending messages in the hope of exercising social influence. Not all her works are as readily invoked in popular culture texts today, through easily accessible allusion, as *Uncle Tom's Cabin* could still be in Turow's *TV Guide* interview. But with that one novel at least, we know that her message was received. *Uncle Tom's Cabin* stands on, even now, as both a monument of American literature and a still-adaptable resource for doing cultural work. It would be surprising if any writer from our own time can stake out a claim to comparable significance, one hundred or so years from now.

Chapter 4

Reception and critics

Stowe was best known during her lifetime as the author of *Uncle Tom's Cabin*, a book outsold in the nineteenth century only by the Bible. For much of the twentieth century, though still having strong name recognition, she virtually disappeared from literary studies and academic publishing. When the recovery of Stowe began in the 1970s, it was framed around *Uncle Tom's Cabin*. Therefore, a history of reception for that text provides a synopsis of Stowe's own shifting place in literary culture.

Early on, "reception" often took the form of appropriation. Given the still loosely developed conceptions of intellectual property and the limited legal authority of copyright in the mid-nineteenth century, Stowe had no control over *Uncle Tom's Cabin*'s rapid absorption into the emerging mass market of commercial culture. For studying Stowe's career today, one benefit of that scenario is that we can draw on the numerous textual products created in response to *Uncle Tom's Cabin* as an indicator of how (and how eagerly) audiences interpreted the text.

Stowe's book quickly inspired a wide range of material culture items capitalizing on the novel's popularity. One dimension of this process literally domesticated the text and its characters. Fans could drink and eat from Uncle Tom-inspired dishes; decorate their homes with wallpaper and knick-knacks depicting scenes from the novel; play with Tom, Eva, and Topsy toys; and perform parlor songs linked to the novel's plot and themes. High-art painters cast tableaux from the novel in oils, while, at the other end of the economic spectrum, cheaply made abridgements heavy on illustration and light on print text made versions of the novel accessible for the youngest of readers. Tom shows took to the stage and later appeared on screen. Preachers' sermons cited the example of Tom's Christian virtues, and, after the Civil War, letters by white women from the north identified the novel as their inspiration for volunteering to teach in southern Reconstruction schools. Overseas, translations abounded, and Stowe herself became an international celebrity. Uncle Tom and the other memorable characters from Stowe's novel seemed to be everywhere, permeating everyday life. Despite this abundance of spin-offs, readers' reactions to the novel varied widely.

US readers' regional differences

In the 1850s, Stowe's novel generated many reviews, crafted from a range of perspectives. To elicit widely varying responses was no more unusual for a bestseller in Stowe's day than it would be today. (For similarly divergent reactions to some novels in Stowe's time, we can look to Nina Baym's *Novels, Readers, and Reviewers*. For comparative purposes, consider the diverse evaluations of Dan Brown's *The Da Vinci Code*, a novel frequently attacked on religious grounds by some readers, praised by others.[1]) What was very unusual, in Stowe's case, was the degree to which reviews of *Uncle Tom's Cabin* promoted an ongoing circuit of textual exchange including the author herself. As outlined in Chapter 3, Stowe wrote *A Key to Uncle Tom's Cabin* to reply to negative assessments of her novel by southern reviewers. The *Key*, in turn, incited another whole spate of angry reviews from the south. Stowe probably had some of those malicious attacks in mind when she skewered the hypocrisy of the southern clergy and legal leaders in *Dred* (1856). The uneasy dialogue would continue in books like Maria McIntosh's *Two Pictures* (1863), where the southern-bred novelist depicts a Georgia plantation couple reading a review of *Uncle Tom's Cabin* in a New York paper and blaming Stowe for causing sectional strife.[2]

As McIntosh's example suggests, written responses to *Uncle Tom's Cabin* varied more markedly by region than by other categories we might use to classify groups of readers, such as gender, social class, or even race. Whereas reviewers from the northern US tended to praise Stowe's book, southerners typically excoriated it. Thomas F. Gossett stresses the intensely negative feelings stirred up by the book and classifies the dominant southern response as "outrage and invective." Pointing out that the somewhat muted assessments appearing in a few southern publications were typically from border states or written by former southerners who had moved to the north, Gossett cites numerous negative reviews that roundly condemn Stowe's portrayal of slave culture as inaccurate to the point of being inflammatory and Stowe herself as having violated all protocols for womanly behavior. For instance, George Frederick Holmes accused her of heresy and a sinful fascination with sex. The novelist William Gilmore Simms ranted in the *Southern Quarterly Review*: "Mrs. Stowe betrays a malignity so remarkable . . . that the petticoat lifts of itself, and we see the hoof of the beast under the table."[3]

A number of the southern responses of *Uncle Tom's Cabin* were written by women, in an apparent effort to cloak attacks on Stowe in a protective cape of feminine propriety. Some of this criticism took the form of irate letters to editors, with self-proclaimed *lady* correspondents occasionally feigning concern about the state of womanhood in America, in light of Stowe's unruly behavior. Clergymen joined in the fray as well, condemning Stowe on religious grounds. Stowe attempted to answer these detractors in the *Key*, where she took particular issue with the charge of unreliability in her depiction of slavery.

Accuracy became the basis for many fictional responses to Stowe's work as well, with a number of opponents writing novels of their own as rejoinders. As Charles F. Briggs noted in a January 1853 review famously entitled "Uncle Tomitudes," this in itself was an amazing phenomenon. Briggs dubbed the explosion of counter-novels "something entirely new in literature," and "one of the most striking testimonials to the intrinsic merit of the work that it should be thought necessary to neutralize its influence by issuing other romances to prove that *Uncle Tom* is a fiction."[4]

Offering alternative portraits of southern life under slavery, these counter-narratives often self-identified as replies to *Uncle Tom's Cabin* through such titles as *Aunt Phillis's Cabin; or, Southern Life as It Is*; *The Cabin and the Parlor, or Slaves and Masters*; and *The Hireling and the Slave*, William J. Grayson's narrative poem idealizing slave culture.[5] Most of these authors self-identified as southerners defending their home region. Some presented themselves like Robert Criswell, who designated his *"Uncle Tom's Cabin" Contrasted with Buckingham Hall, The Planter's Home* as composed by a northerner who had "travelled extensively through the South" and therefore had acquired a "fair and impartial" perspective on slavery – an obvious reference to Stowe's own shortage of first-hand knowledge and her purported exaggerations of slavery's abuses.[6]

When surveying what have tended to be labeled as *southern response novels*, we do need to keep in mind that "southern" is a complicated category to invoke, in this context. Many of the novels were, as suggested above, written by southerners and published in the southern US, but others were composed by pro-slavery southern sympathizers living in the north. For instance, the transplanted Georgian Maria McIntosh, who lived in New York, first wrote a long letter to the editor of the *Observer* in her adopted city to protest English women's misunderstanding of slavery, as expressed in their embrace of Stowe during the author's first trip abroad. McIntosh then turned to fiction, pouring out *The Lofty and the Lowly*, a multi-volume saga portraying kindly southerners viewing beloved slaves as family members. Meanwhile, the personal geography for Caroline Lee Hentz, living in the south in the 1850s, was even more complicated in relation to Stowe. Hentz had previously lived in Cincinnati, overlapping with the Beechers' tenure there, and she had belonged to the same Semicolon literary club that had nurtured Stowe's early writing. Despite their common experience in the west – or perhaps because of it – these two women writers were very much on opposite sides of north/south sectional strife once Hentz began replying in fiction to Stowe's first novel.

Besides authors' locations being complicated to classify, sites of production were complex for the "southern" response books. With the northeast still the center of the book-making industry, it was more likely that an anti-Tom novel would be published there than in Charleston. One Philadelphia publisher, the respected J. B. Lippincott, brought out over a half-dozen. (Philadelphia itself was ambiguously positioned, being home to both transplanted southerners and sympathizers with cross-regional business interests.) In addition, the "southern" novels were quickly internationalized. One London firm handled both Stowe's *A Key to Uncle Tom's Cabin* and Charles Jacobs Peterson's *Cabin and Parlour*.

Revisions of Tom were, of course, central to the anti-Tom novels and their heirs, but other characters also claimed the attention of counter-narrative authors. Though Stowe's *Key* indicates she had tried to create some appealing southern characters, some southern readers even found figures like Mrs Shelby aggravating, citing such details as her failure to sympathize soon enough with Eliza's plight. Marie St Clare, meanwhile, infuriated southern audiences.

Because one of their goals was to counteract such characterizations, as well as to resist components of her plot, the southern response novels tended to be dependent upon Stowe's text for features in their content. For instance, in the anti-Tom novels, scenes paralleling the escape attempts in *Uncle Tom's Cabin* depict slaves being captured by abolitionists and carried off to the north – an ironic twist on Stowe's goal of critiquing the Fugitive Slave Law in the first place. Similarly, as a counter to Stowe's focus on Tom's learning to read – and especially to study his Bible – an anti-Tom novel might offer an extended scene of black slaves' oral story-telling, cast in a humorous tone and exaggerated dialect that simultaneously insisted on their inability to be educated. (See, for instance, the minstrelsy-oriented conversation between Jeff and Uncle Pete in Criswell's *Buckingham Hall*, pp. 63–5).

While a few anti-Tom authors, like Criswell, claimed to be mediating between Stowe and her novel's opponents, many freely vented their wrath.

And significantly, that anger did not subside over time. Though appearing in 1892, Annie Jefferson Holland's *The Refugees: A Sequel to "Uncle Tom's Cabin"* testified to the staying power of southerners' resentment, years after the Civil War and Reconstruction had ended. Asserting that "'The Refugees' is a story composed of real facts, a chain of authentic instances" to serve as a corrective to Stowe's novel, Holland invoked the familiar charge of unreliability against *Uncle Tom's Cabin*, explaining that this new narrative on southern life, unlike Stowe's, had been prepared by "A Southern woman, who lived through it, knowing it as it was and is." Holland declared: "It was not strange for a woman, with an overwrought religious temperament, to have written 'Uncle Tom's Cabin,' but it was strange that the whole world accepted it as true ... No one seemed to have any idea of the civilizing effect of slavery, and that at its very worst it was far better for the negro than Africa." Calling on readers to reject Stowe's "superstition and fanaticism," Holland hoped her own story, by "resurrect[ing]" Uncle Tom, would counter the earlier novel's lingering cultural power.[7]

For Holland, writing near a new century, *Uncle Tom's Cabin* still stood out as a lying assault on the south. And she was not alone in trying to carve out a different perspective on antebellum southern life decades after the novel's first publication, for a notable number of white writers would revisit material from Stowe's novel to re-envision their region's history after Reconstruction had passed. More famously than Holland, for instance, Thomas Dixon drew on material from *Uncle Tom's Cabin* and from the anti-Tom novels when writing *The Leopard's Spots: A Romance of the White Man's Burden 1865–1900* (1903) and *The Clansman: An Historical Romance of the Ku Klux Klan* (1905). Dixon's novels, in turn, would be the basis for D. W. Griffith's *The Birth of a Nation* (1906), a film whose technical wizardry set new standards, but whose racist stance is traceable back to the anti-Tom novels of the 1850s.

For Dixon and Griffith, critiquing what they perceived as ongoing race-based abuses of southern whites entailed re-writing history. Specifically, after attending a 1901 performance of one of the "Tom plays" still quite popular in the early twentieth century, Dixon determined to create an alternative portrait of the south's past. When we read Dixon's novels and view Griffith's film with a knowledge of Stowe's novel and the original 1850s counter-narratives as part of our interpretive context, we can see how the imagery and associated ideology behind *Birth of a Nation*'s clansmen "heroes" and its frighteningly brutish black men have antecedents in Stowe and the anti-Tom texts. And recognition of such links between *Birth of a Nation*'s racist constructions of black male identity and conflicts around *Uncle Tom's Cabin*'s reception certainly resonates with race issues still not resolved in America today. For example, as Linda Williams has noted, Griffith's film was intent upon replacing the sympathy-inducing scenes

of Uncle Tom being victimized (as in stage plays and early films drawn from
Stowe's novel) with the figure of a black male endangering an innocent white
woman. This alternative melodrama would help justify the ongoing oppression
of black men in the south at the turn into the twentieth century. Reinvigorating
the very arguments that had been mounted against Stowe's vision of southern
black–white relations in the original round of anti-Tom novels of the 1850s,
Dixon and Griffith sought to suppress the political interventions associated
with Reconstruction.[8]

Later, if more romantically, Margaret Mitchell's 1930s novel *Gone with the
Wind* and its film version would also tap into the reservoir of cultural memory
associated with Stowe's text and its resistant heirs. As these ongoing reverbera-
tions recur even today throughout popular culture, the degree to which Stowe's
novel tapped into deeply felt social relations is continually evident.

Despite the persistent tendency of southerners to attack *Uncle Tom's Cabin*,
some read the novel with a more open mind, and a few even found the text
worthy of praise. In 1853, F. C. Adams published an entire book reporting
on the perspectives of southern readers, a number of whom he depicted as
appreciating the novel. Titled *Uncle Tom at Home: A Review of the Reviewers
and Repudiators of Uncle Tom's Cabin by Mrs. Stowe*, Adams's book announces
itself as a defense: "We have taken up the book upon its merits in answer to those
who have preceded us upon its demerits." Calling the vocal "adversaries" of
Uncle Tom's Cabin "violent," Adams signs himself as writing from Charleston
and insists that "we know there are many good Southerners who do not dif-
fer with our opinions" – either on slavery or on its depiction by Stowe. Adams
offers anecdotal accounts of discussing the book, particularly its degree of truth
in portraying slavery's ills. He pokes fun at the way that some southern readers
sent up hue and cry against Stowe without reading the novel, then describes
how one "gentleman of the legal profession," known for his "literary discrimi-
nation," admitted to having admired its "ease and natural simplicity," despite
finding that "some of its scenes [were] rather highly coloured." In contrast
with assertions that Stowe had overdrawn slavery's abuses, Adams declares:
"she could not have delineated them with more truthfulness." Citing one local
southerner's affirmation that Legree had a direct parallel in "Thomas L–e on
James Island, South Carolina," Adams declares that she "could not have drawn
a more admirable portrait," and suggests that "good masters" do not want to
admit that they recognize her portrayals of abuse as "truthful." Adams also
includes a point-by-point refutation of one especially brutal southern review,
by a Mr. Simms (probably William Gilmore Simms, whose battering of Stowe
had already become legendary). To highlight the unfairness of Simms's attack,
Adams repeatedly cites real-life cases that match scenes Stowe had constructed

and Simms had critiqued. Overall, Adams intones, "This is the preeminent point in Mrs. Stowe's book – to show Southerners that they neglect their own interests." Although Adams acknowledges that the opprobrium hurled at the novel has come mainly from the south, he also criticizes northern readers who have defended slavery rather than supporting Stowe. "These latter," he observes, "with Godey and Graham's goodly numbers combined, have assumed the sponsorship" of slavery, through "motives" Adams says he cannot understand. (One of Adams's targets here could be Sarah Josepha Hale, the editor of *Godey's Lady's Book*, who had chosen *not* to review *Uncle Tom's Cabin* – whereas she printed enthusiastic reports on anti-Tom books – and who censured Stowe's *Key* when it appeared.) Characterizing himself (a voice from the south) as a counterpoint to those misguided northern pro-slavery apologists, Adams hypothesizes that many more southerners recognize "the simple truth" of Stowe's narrative than care to admit it.[9]

Adams does not offer specific audience data, however, and reports on reception in the south tend to be anecdotal, as when northern travelers describe seeing the book in stores or observing individuals reading it. That there were plenty of readers in the north is easier to verify, based on the publisher's record of selling 300,000 copies within the first year. And while Stowe's novel drew intense attacks from southerners, the book claimed numerous vocal admirers in the north. Even literary luminaries – including Ralph Waldo Emerson, James Russell Lowell and Henry Wadsworth Longfellow – praised the book.

Some treatments of *Uncle Tom's Cabin*'s antebellum readership in the north have lumped this enormous audience together as if all that region's readers were universally enthusiastic. Actually, despite the very positive response in that region overall, there were exceptions. Naysayers took their stand for a range of reasons. A few, in an early sign of prejudice against the growth of mass culture, turned up their noses at the book's very popularity. Some regretted its potential for undermining the union; others complained that its condemnation of slavery and assertions of black humanity did not go far enough.

Antebellum blacks as readers

Marva Banks has outlined shifting, diverse perspectives in the reactions of African American readers, and these distinctions resonate with questions about race and the novel that continue to draw attention today. One notable point is the sheer quantity of blacks' public responses. According to Banks, at least two hundred articles appeared between 1852 and 1855 in over a half-dozen publications, with *Frederick Douglass' Paper* printing many of these pieces.

Another is the tendency of these responses to situate the text within a framework of larger social issues (such as employment and education) rather than around the narrative itself. Furthermore, Banks observes, blacks' reactions to the text changed over time. Initially, most leaders – including William Still, William Wells Brown and Frederick Douglass – appreciated the novel's contribution as propaganda. The African American exile William Craft even wrote approvingly from England about the impact the novel was having there on the anti-slavery movement. Yet, Banks declares, antebellum black leaders became increasingly vocal about the novel's racist stereotypes and its troubling affirmation of the colonization movement.[10]

Even as he was praising *Uncle Tom's Cabin* as a forceful weapon in the fight against slavery, Frederick Douglass was also campaigning against the colonization crusade. Correspondence between Douglass and Stowe during the writing of *Uncle Tom's Cabin* shows that she was trying to persuade him to reconsider his position on the issue. It was Stowe, however, who eventually moderated her stance. Just a few years later, she did not send any of her characters in *Dred* to Africa, as she had done with her first anti-slavery novel. In the time between the two texts' publication moments, she had encountered increasing criticism from black leaders over her pro-colonization stand in *Uncle Tom's Cabin*. For instance, the black leader George T. Downing had urged delegates attending an anti-slavery convention to denounce the novel's pro-colonization stance, and William G. Allen had sent a letter to *Frederick Douglass' Paper* expressing a similar position. In the fall of 1852, Douglass himself wrote an editorial critiquing the novel's final chapters in these terms.

Several months afterward, Martin Delany submitted an even more forceful condemnation to Douglass's periodical, with the colonization issue a major complaint. Delany also called Stowe to task for broader failings, including the presumption that she could speak for all African Americans: "she knows nothing about us, the free colored people of the United States," asserted Delany. This charge led to a series of letters between Douglass and Delany, with the former defending Stowe, despite her novel's stand on colonization, as a supporter of abolition. "We recognize friends wherever we find them," Douglass insisted. For the pragmatic Douglass, "the brief letter by George Harris, at the close of Uncle Tom's Cabin" could not "vitiate forever, Mrs. Stowe's power to do us good." Douglass's advocacy aside, other African American leaders joined Delany in critiquing *Uncle Tom's Cabin*, not just over colonization itself but also for the racist attitudes behind Stowe's position on this issue and her depiction of black characters. Central to such grievances, then and now, has been the novel's title character. C. L. Redmond, William G. Nell, William J. Wilson, The Reverend J. B. Smith, and George T. Downing were just a few of the US-based black leaders forcefully objecting to Stowe's depiction of Tom as overly submissive. Their position was extended by a correspondent writing for the Canadian paper the *Provincial Freeman*, who demanded that Uncle Tom be "killed" off as a racist image of subservience.[11]

Like the southern readers whose negative responses to Stowe's text included both assaults against its failings and new anti-Tom books, free blacks in the north offered their critiques in both reviews and narratives of their own. But if these contemporary African American responses to *Uncle Tom's Cabin* shared some genre traits with southern ones, they certainly differed in important ways – including highlighting a contrasting set of charges against Stowe. Furthermore, in their tendency to combine some appreciation of her rhetorical skill with identification of her shortcomings, blacks' counter-narratives also had a far more complex relationship with *Uncle Tom's Cabin* than whites'. In that regard, the creative moves many African American writers have made to exert authority over the novel, beginning as early as the 1850s, testify that, despite Toni Morrison's observation that *Uncle Tom's Cabin* was not "written for Uncle Tom to read or be persuaded by,"[12] the text has held a very productive place in black literary culture.

Consistent with the objections raised in reviews, African American response narratives written during Stowe's day often focused on revising her characterization of black manhood. In that vein, Frederick Douglass's repeated praise of Stowe and her novel in his speeches and in the press should be read alongside his construction of Madison Washington in the novella "The Heroic Slave," which was part of a fund-raising project for *Frederick Douglass' Paper* in 1852. Douglass's hero offers a very different portrait of black male agency than *Uncle Tom's Cabin*. After an initial escape to the north, Douglass's character boldly returns south to rescue his wife, and eventually settles in the New-World setting of a British Caribbean island (the Bahamas) rather than in Africa. In addition, unlike Stowe, who attributes George Harris's assertiveness to the white side of his identity and associates Uncle Tom's docility with his pure blackness, Douglass directly associates his central character's heroism with blackness. As Robert Stepto explains, Douglass's revision of Tom is a savvy one, taking an additive approach that builds on the character's best traits rather than fully repudiating him.[13]

Douglass's counter-narrative to *Uncle Tom's Cabin* helped inaugurate what would, in effect, become a whole sub-genre in American literature, black male authors' refutations of Uncle Tom – a far different "anti-Tom" tradition than that coming out of the white south. For instance, William Wells Brown's *Clotel; or, The President's Daughter* powerfully addressed several issues at the heart of African Americans' responses to *Uncle Tom's Cabin*, including questions about miscegenation and the colonization movement's impact on US race relations. In Brown's narrative a George Green character serves up a direct contrast to George Harris's rejection of America and move to Africa, since Green calls for a multiracial America and supports black revolt, if needed, to claim rights associated with the Declaration of Independence. Along similar lines, Martin Delany's *Blake; or, the Huts of America* (originally serialized in 1859) can be read as rejecting even the more radical position Stowe would take on black violence in her second anti-slavery novel, *Dred*. For Delany, *Blake* would suggest, even *Dred* did not go far enough in its depiction of righteous black insurrection. By organizing slaves throughout the American south, as well as in his revolutionary leadership in Cuba, Delany's Henry Holland (also known as Blacus and Blake) is a more extreme version of Stowe's Dred, and light years removed from the stalwart Christian passivity of Uncle Tom.

African American antebellum narratives like *Clotel* and *Blake* had a far more complicated relationship with *Uncle Tom's Cabin* than did the southern pro-slavery response fiction being produced by whites. Southern anti-Tom novels were constructed as direct rejections of Stowe's argument and, therefore, were dependent upon her story for their very conception. In contrast, African American texts "responding" to *Uncle Tom's Cabin* were also affiliating with a rich, pre-existent tradition of black American culture that Stowe herself had drawn upon – particularly the autobiographical narratives that were already being written by escaped slaves like Frederick Douglass, whose life story had been published in 1845. Accordingly, Peter A. Dorsey has focused on connections between *Uncle Tom's Cabin* and *Clotel* to highlight the interactive relationship between Stowe's novel and African American literature. While noting that each author borrowed from the other (Stowe from Brown's slavery narrative for her novel, then Brown from Stowe's novel for his), Dorsey credits Stowe with expanding the generic range of anti-slavery narratives beyond biographical texts. But Dorsey also shows that her claims for the realism of her novel were possible only because of the already established tradition of personal histories written by African Americans themselves – which Stowe used to resist critics' positioning of *Uncle Tom's Cabin* as a romance, and therefore untrustworthy.[14]

Keeping such ongoing intertextuality in mind, we should note that Harriet Beecher Stowe certainly borrowed from antebellum African American literature and culture more than she inspired it. In her *Key*, for example, she admitted having taken many of the ideas for her plotline and characterization of Uncle Tom from the life experience of Josiah Henson. In addition, during the composition of the initial serial, she was corresponding with Frederick Douglass, seeking his input. Stowe also drew a number of elements from the narrative of Henry Bibb, including descriptions of plantation life and of escaping north by crossing the Ohio River, as Eliza Harris does in *Uncle Tom's Cabin.*

Commenting sardonically upon the seeming ease with which Stowe appropriated blacks' lived experience, Ishmael Reed would playfully return the favor in *Flight to Canada* (1976). There, in presenting a sustained parodic re-working of her themes, he would charge Stowe with literary theft of Josiah Henson's life:

> Uncle Tom's Cabin. *Writing is strange, though. That story caught up with her. The story she "borrowed" from Josiah Henson. Harriet only wanted enough money to buy a silk dress. The paper mills ground day and night. She'd read Josiah Henson's book. That Harriet was alert.* The Life of Josiah Henson, Formerly a Slave. *Seventy-seven pages long. It was short, but it was his. It was all he had. His story. A man's story is his gris-gris, you know. Taking his story is like taking his gris-gris. The thing that is himself. It's like robbing a man of his Etheric Double.*[15]

In Stowe's own day, being strategic within available spaces for their writing, African American writers and their promoters were often likely to affiliate their texts with her famous bestseller rather than to complain about her use of black cultural capital to design her story in the first place. Along those lines, the 1853 London edition of *Clotel; or, The President's Daughter* folded into the autobiographical narrative William Wells Brown used to introduce his novel an enthusiastic quote from *The Eclectic*: "The extraordinary excitement produced by 'Uncle Tom's Cabin' will, we hope, prepare the public of Great Britain and America for this lively book of travels by a real fugitive."[16] Aligning Brown's text with Stowe's (through the hope that her success would draw readers to his) and yet also distancing his narrative from hers (with the implicit contrast between Tom's imagined story and Brown's life as "a real fugitive slave"), this allusion marked the complex interplay between *Uncle Tom's Cabin* and many other African American literary productions during Stowe's lifetime.

If Stowe borrowed (or stole) from Henson, Bibb, and others, their literary heirs would build on those connections, both economically and artistically. A telling example of the complexity in these relationships, which sometimes had a personal as well as an intertextual dimension, has emerged from research on Harriet Jacobs, author of *Incidents in the Life of a Slave Girl* (1861). Jacobs's personal narrative included an important counter-point to Stowe's characters' emigration to Africa, since a good deal of *Incidents* focuses on "Linda Brent" becoming established in the north after her escape – claiming a social space within the US rather than leaving the nation behind. But there were also complicated interpersonal connections between the two women writers that make the contrasts in their accounts all the more striking.

As Jean Yellin's meticulous recovery of Jacobs's history has shown, Harriet Beecher Stowe both enabled and constrained Jacobs's search for a literary voice. Although Jacobs had been nervous about reporting on her personal life in the south, by 1852–3 she was hoping that a record of her experiences might support the anti-slavery cause. Yellin's study of Jacobs's correspondence with her white friend Amy Post highlights Jacobs's efforts to secure Stowe's assistance for telling the compelling life story that would eventually appear under Jacobs's pseudonym of Linda Brent.

Feeling insecure about writing an autobiography, but encouraged by a number of supporters to do so, Jacobs first envisioned collaborating with Stowe, provided the by-then-well-known author of *Uncle Tom's Cabin* could be recruited. But Jacobs's idealistic vision of cooperative story-telling disintegrated in the face of a dismissive response from Stowe, who wanted not to collaborate but to incorporate details from Jacobs's life in *A Key to Uncle Tom's Cabin*. Jacobs's patron Mrs Cornelia Willis then wrote another letter to Stowe, requesting that the bestselling author refrain from using Jacobs's material, in accordance with a goal Jacobs herself would explain to Amy Post: "that I wished it to be a history of my life entirely by itself." Stowe's failure to respond to this request, coupled with prior insults to Jacobs and her daughter Louisa, wound up having an effect that the author of *Uncle Tom's Cabin* probably never anticipated. Angry over Stowe's behavior, Jacobs became more committed to anti-slavery writing herself. Jacobs soon made her first foray into the field by sending a letter to the editor of the *Tribune*, responding to a pro-slavery article. After receiving positive feedback, she submitted another contribution a month later, signing her piece "Fugitive." In October of 1853, Jacobs wrote to Amy Post outlining a plan to write what would become *Incidents in the Life of a Slave Girl*. Referencing the frustrating experience with Stowe, but also the lift her *Tribune* pieces had provided, Jacobs declared: "I must write just what I have lived and witnessed myself . . ."[17]

Not all the antebellum African American authors whose work was shaped by Stowe experienced her influence in such negative terms, personally, as Jacobs had. Frances E. W. Harper used *Uncle Tom's Cabin* as an inspiration for poetry. At least three of her early poems – "Eliza Harris," "To Harriet Beecher Stowe," and "Eva's Farewell" – were directly linked to Harper's reading of the novel and were well received when published in abolitionist periodicals.[18] By 1854, Harper had gained enough recognition to publish *Poems on Miscellaneous Subjects*, with Boston and Philadelphia editions, both of which sold very well. Extending her lecture career into the south after the Civil War, Harper also expanded her body of printed literary works to include narratives reexamining themes from anti-slavery writing. Two of these in particular – *Minnie's Sacrifice* (1869) and the more mature *Iola Leroy, or Shadows Uplifted* (1892) – offer additional evidence of how productively Stowe's texts would continue to interact with African Americans' writing, well beyond the antebellum era. Harper's confident reworkings of genre conventions Stowe had used also demonstrate that, however often they might revisit material linked to *Uncle Tom's Cabin*, black American authors would also assert their own authority over such literary traditions. Along those lines, *Iola Leroy* became the best-selling book by a black author in its time period. In Harper's case, indeed, we see a woman writer whose career had a length, productiveness, and range comparable to Stowe's, but who continued to focus on race issues long after Stowe had shifted her emphasis to other topics.

African American authors writing in the post-Reconstruction/pre-Harlem Renaissance era, as Harper did at the end of her career, still faced a challenge in relation to Stowe's abiding influence. A residue of literary memory lingered in the larger culture as a result of Stowe's forceful characterizations of blacks (ranging from her comic figures like Topsy, to her differentiating between pure blacks and mulattos, not to mention her hyper-Christian Tom). These formed a binding framework into which African American authors often struggled to fit their work. Thus, Richard Yarborough indicates, novels like James H. W. Howard's *Bond and Free: A True Tale of Slave Times* (1886), Walter H. Stowers's and William H. Anderson's *Appointed* (1894), and both Harper's *Iola Leroy* and Victoria Earle's *Aunt Lindy: A Story Founded on Real Life* (1892) were at least somewhat constrained by the persistent legacy of Stowe's characters, her ideas about race, and her views on how blacks should respond to oppression.[19]

African Americans' responses in a new century

Throughout the twentieth century, African American literature maintained a highly interactive relationship with Stowe and *Uncle Tom's Cabin*. Black male authors, in particular, repeatedly turned their attention to revising Uncle Tom. At the turn into the 1900s, for example, Charles Chesnutt cannily reconfigured the Tom stereotype into the cagey Uncle Julius in a series of "conjure" stories, a number of which initially appeared in *Atlantic Monthly* (a regular publishing venue for Stowe) before being collected in *The Conjure Woman* anthology (1899). Readers versed in Uncle Tom's evolving characterization into an ineffectual old man, as the audience for the *Atlantic* would have been, were well equipped to see how Julius renegotiated that role. Julius's strategic use of language, based in trickster folk tales, reasserted control over the relationship between blacks and would-be white authority figures like Chesnutt's white northern transplant John. In the opening decades of the century, the ongoing exchanges between W. E. B. DuBois and Booker T. Washington tapped into the Stowe-shaped cultural resource of audiences' expectations about black male leadership. Washington's approaches to accommodating whites' perspectives were sometimes classified as "Uncle Tom" behavior, and DuBois's questions about blacks' education and pan-Africanism called for African Americans' agency in areas that had been associated with Stowe's George Harris.

In the 1920s, as some black leaders were urging more assertive responses to racism, the Uncle Tom figure remained readily available as an apt point of reference. For instance, a 1925 essay in *Frederick Douglass' Paper* called on the Tom stereotype to persuade African American Pullman porters to join the union movement. Complaining that the "handicap under which the porters [were then] laboring" was "due to the fact that there [were] too many Uncle Toms in the service," A. Philip Randolph urged pullmen to leave behind a "slave psychology" which led them to "bow and kowtow and lick the boots of the Company officials, who either pity or despise them."[20]

In the 1930s, Richard Wright wrote *Uncle Tom's Children*, whose title signaled that the stories collected there would present the perspective of a different black generation than the one portrayed by Stowe. Indeed, Wright announced in his epigraph for the stories, "The post Civil War household word among Negroes – 'He's an Uncle Tom!' . . . has been supplanted by a new word from another generation which says: – 'Uncle Tom is dead!' "[21] The 1940 edition of Wright's anthology added the scathing autobiographical essay "The Ethics of Jim Crow," where Wright responded to reviewers' questions about the reliability of his accounts in *Uncle Tom's Children* by making as adept a use of bitter irony as Stowe had in her *Key* coda to the 1850s novel. Later, as James Baldwin noted in his seminal 1949 essay on *Uncle Tom's Cabin* (see below), Wright's Bigger Thomas in *Native Son* could be read as an even more overt assault on Stowe's version of black manhood.

A number of African American women authors would put *Uncle Tom's Cabin* in its place by claiming black authority for writing about slavery. Sherley Anne Williams (*Dessa Rose*), Octavia Butler (*Kindred*), and Toni Morrison (*Beloved*), among others, would revisit themes from Stowe's *Uncle Tom's Cabin*, while more determinedly affiliating their neo-anti-slavery novels with the tradition of black writers like Harriet Jacobs, Frederick Douglass, and Frances Harper. Blending celebration of black literary traditions with traces of Stowe's lingering legacy, such texts point to the ways in which African American and white literary culture continue to interact.

If, as Toni Morrison suggests, "the Africanist character as surrogate and enabler" has been at the heart of American literature's development – including, and perhaps especially, that literature written by whites – then surely *Uncle Tom's Cabin* has been a prime example of the process through which white writers have used black characters so that "the American [white] self knows itself as not enslaved, but free; not repulsive, but desirable; not helpless, but licensed and powerful; not history-less, but historical; not damned, but innocent; not a blind accident of evolution but a progressive fulfillment of destiny."[22] In playing that role to the hilt, Stowe's novel has also carried out a persistent haunting of black literature – leaving a set of ghosts to be reckoned with, even when not overtly engaged.

Along those lines, in his memoir-cum-analysis *Turning South Again: Rethinking Modernism/Re-reading Booker T.*, we see the scholar-artist Houston A. Baker repeatedly referencing both W. E. B. DuBois and Booker T. Washington, as well as Baker's own experiences growing up in the south, in ways that also mark a linkage of black literary culture to Harriet Beecher Stowe, even today. Describing his family's travels across the Ohio from Louisville ("my Old Kentucky Home") into a temporary haven of integration; reconsidering the figure of the "Yankee schoolmarm" in Washington's depictions of Mrs Viola Ruffner, along with the theme of white-sponsored and white-impeded literacy acquisition; revisiting his own readings of "writers like Ralph Ellison, Richard Wright, James Baldwin, and Booker T. Washington" in search of a more "millennial standpoint" – in all these moves Baker simultaneously celebrates the liberatory possibilities now open to black Americans in the south and acknowledges, if only implicitly, traces of Stowe's cultural influence.[23] So too, in the introductory "Autobiographical Notes" for the same text where he published his famous "Everybody's Protest Novel" critique of Stowe, James Baldwin identified *Uncle Tom's Cabin*, with *A Tale of Two Cities*, as a book he read in his youth, "over and over and over again."[24]

Nineteenth-century European responses

Uncle Tom's Cabin was an unprecedented success in the antebellum US, but it was even more of a phenomenon in Europe. It was quickly translated into numerous languages, with editions prepared for juvenile as well as adult readers. In a reverse of what had been the predominant pattern – American readers eagerly buying works by English writers like Dickens – Stowe's text became a European sensation.

French packagings of the novel, like English ones, drew from and shaped popular perceptions about life in America. These European versions sometimes reconfigured features of plot and characterization to highlight a particular translation's vision of US culture. Stowe's friend Annie Fields cited evidence of the book's immense popularity in Europe by documenting the impulse to produce multiple versions in French, for a range of different audiences. Fields reports that Madame L. S. Belloc, who had also translated works by the British author Maria Edgeworth, was invited by one French publisher to prepare what would become the fifth translation of *Uncle Tom's Cabin*. When Belloc protested that perhaps there were already enough versions available, the publisher, M. Charpentier, is said to have replied: "Il n'y aura jamais assez de lecteurs pour un tel livre," or "There can never be enough readers for a book such as this." According to Madame Belloc, his confidence was rewarded, when "La Case de l'Oncle Tom" was successful enough to prompt a sixth, illustrated edition only a few months later. Declared Belloc: "It was read by high and low, by grown persons and children. A great enthusiasm for the anti-slavery cause was the result. The popularity of the work in France was immense, and no doubt influenced the public mind in favor of the North during the war of secession" (qtd in Fields, *Life and Letters*, pp. 157–8).

One of the most enthusiastic reviews of *Uncle Tom's Cabin* ever written was by the French author Amandine Aurore Lucile Dupin, who regularly published under the pseudonym of George Sand. Sand expressed unabashed admiration for Stowe's novel in terms that simultaneously served as an impassioned defense of that most feminine of literary modes – sentimentalism. But the review is also important to literary history as a sign of Stowe's enormous popularity in Europe. Sand described *Uncle Tom's Cabin* as being "in all hands and in all journals," to the extent that "[i]t is not longer permissible to those who can read not to have read it." Underscoring the intensity of audiences' reactions, she declared that "people devour it, they cover it with tears." Though a highly successful novelist herself, Sand insisted that the only proper response to Stowe would be "a homage," and the French author even imagined men, women, and children of "this old world" "cross[ing] the seas . . . to say to her that she is esteemed and beloved!"[25]

Nowhere around the globe did Stowe's novel generate a more enthusiastic response than in England. The first British edition, pirated by the Clarke firm of London, appeared just two months after the Boston one, and the term "Tom Mania," signifying the wild enthusiasm for the text that dominated much of the nineteenth century, was actually coined in London. Whereas approximately 300,000 copies of the novel were sold in America in the first year, the same time period generated sales of well over one million in Britain. The degree to which

England embraced Stowe's novel can be measured in part by an early British edition's boasting the same illustrator employed for Charles Dickens's books, George Cruikshank.[26]

Painters created fine art based in imagery associated with *Uncle Tom's Cabin* – including works by Edwin Long, Louisa Corbaux, F. S. Cary, G. P. Manley, and Anna Blunder. Although some well-known reviewers (such as Thomas Carlyle, Matthew Arnold, and William Makepeace Thackery) found the novel to be inexpertly crafted, Stowe garnered many positive notices as well. Significantly, *Uncle Tom's Cabin* attracted British readers across all social classes. The novel was studied in middle-class Sunday schools, performed in working-class playhouses, and championed by the nobility and the political elite. William Gladstone gave away copies to prostitutes on street corners in the hope that reading it would help them reform.

British readers actively integrated the novel into their ideas about life in the Americas, and the novel also shaped those views. For instance, the former slave Josiah Henson's fame became tightly bound up with his links to the character of Uncle Tom. English audiences had previously embraced Henson's *Autobiography*, published in Europe before *Uncle Tom's Cabin*, and had welcomed his participation in the Great Exhibition of 1851 to tout the progress of his community in Canada. But when he returned to Britain in the 1870s, after becoming closely identified with Stowe's Tom, Henson received the fullest celebrity treatment, even being presented to Queen Victoria. Henson himself objected to the confusion of his identity with Tom's, complaining that people had "forgotten that Mrs Stowe's *Uncle Tom's Cabin* is a novel," in which the hero died, whereas he, Josiah Henson, was very much alive, with his own name and identity.[27] Yet the press persisted in presenting Henson as a touring Uncle Tom, thereby affirming both England's continued fascination with Stowe's novel and a tendency to read it uncritically as a straightforward portrait of life in North America. Indeed, the explosive popularity of the novel among British and continental readers drew from and fed their longing to explore – if only vicariously – a vision of America made accessible through literature.

If for some English readers *Uncle Tom's Cabin* was most appealing as an "American" story, for others the text was most significant as a political call to arms. In the 1850s, enthusiasm over the novel led to increased membership in British anti-slavery societies, including enhanced participation by the aristocracy. It prompted the famous Stafford House address, a proclamation of opposition to slavery signed by half a million women and presented to Stowe during her first trip to Europe. From the perspective of US southerners, the petition was alarming, both as a mark of Britain's upper crust joining a movement that had been associated with middle-class dissenters (i.e., Protestants not affiliated with the Church of England) and, even more so, as an indication of that country's now potentially favoring the US north over the south in the ongoing slavery debate.

Stowe's first trip abroad, sponsored by the Glasgow Ladies' New Anti-Slavery Society, raised some eyebrows for the abundance of gifts given to her to compensate for royalties lost to the pirated British editions. Stowe was criticized personally for her enthusiastic cultivation of the British aristocracy. That stance seemed at odds with her republican American background and her supposedly unselfish dedication to lowly slaves. Especially galling to some was Stowe's eager affiliation with the Duchess of Sutherland, whose family had a history of abusing their tenants in earlier generations. Stowe's willingness to capitalize personally on her novel's success in England seemed inconsistent with her purported reasons for writing the narrative in the first place – to speak in a pure Christian voice against an immoral social practice.

Frederick Douglass defended Stowe against charges that she was using her first European trip to line her own pockets. He predicted that resources she gathered there would be donated to support the education of former slaves. Douglass's hopes were dashed. Instead, what benefited most from the immense popularity of *Uncle Tom's Cabin* in England and from Stowe's European journeys? Her own professional writing career.

Overall, Stowe's first visit to the British Isles exemplified her increasingly sophisticated management of her authorship in an era when the conventions for international marketing of literature that so permeate our culture today were not yet in place. Like the book tours authors regularly undertake now, Stowe's first journey to England was designed in large part as self-promotion, and the trip was highly successful in those terms. When Stowe and the cluster of Beecher family members with her first arrived in Liverpool in April of 1853, she found the entire dock literally lined with fans (Hedrick, *HBS*, p. 233).

Throughout her visit, Stowe would be treated like some international celebrity activists (such as the band U2 or Angelina Jolie) have been in the twenty-first century, touted for both her social conscience and her talent, with salutes to one continually reinforcing her fans' belief in the other. Constrained from speaking publicly herself because of her gender, when at the numerous events honoring her and the novel, Stowe often sat like a queen giving audience to courtiers as her husband Calvin or her brother Charles read prepared remarks for her. Along the way, she met a whole array of aristocrats and literary celebrities who would become a part of her growing international network for promoting her future writing. Meanwhile, the publicity associated with the trip spurred sales of *Uncle Tom's Cabin* both abroad and in the US.

Twentieth-century literary criticism

In the final decades of the twentieth century, scholars produced extensive work on Harriet Beecher Stowe. Beginning with reevaluations of *Uncle Tom's Cabin* and expanding, gradually, to explore her other writings, this still-growing body of research has reclaimed a central position for Stowe in literary history. On one level, Stowe's temporary displacement from the canon is a bit puzzling, given the ways in which her most familiar novel has continued to exercise obvious influences on American culture. On the other hand, her literary reputation was doomed to encounter challenges by virtue of that very appeal.

In the early twentieth century, although the icon of Uncle Tom was actively circulating in popular culture, Stowe and her authorship were virtually ignored by academic critics – except as points of reference to denigrate un-aesthetic writing aimed at mass audiences. In the US, when the New Criticism's value system rose in favor, the place of writers like Stowe in literary history declined in direct proportion to increasing interest in high-art texts. One dimension of the early twentieth-century move to exclude works from the canon on this basis involved dismissing publications by nineteenth-century women writers. Along with Catharine Maria Sedgwick, Susan Warner, Maria Cummins, Lydia Maria Child, Lydia Sigourney and others, Stowe was relegated to the "damned mob of scribbling women" Nathaniel Hawthorne had famously criticized in the mid-1800s for a purported lack of commitment to artistic achievement.

In contrast, whereas Herman Melville had been frustrated by the cultural capital women writers were claiming in the nineteenth century, he and others whose work fit the expectations of formalist aesthetics achieved a rise in their fortunes in academic circles through the first half of the twentieth. Accordingly, as Eric Sundquist pointed out, "Many major critical studies of American litera-ture in [the twentieth] century [found] no place for Stowe"; she was frequently excluded from considerations of the antebellum era sometimes dubbed "the American Renaissance," and the "polemicism and sentimentality" that had so attracted readers in the 1850s became the target of critique. Thus, Sundquist explains, for much of the twentieth century, academic readers judged Stowe's work as suffering from being "awkwardly plotted, overly melodramatic, and naively visionary," to the point of "wallow[ing] in tears."[28]

The *entrée* women scholars gained into humanities fields of the academy in the late twentieth century – supported by the larger movement of feminism – led to a reexamination of the literary canon on gendered grounds. Stowe and other women writers of her day benefited from this reevaluation, even when it included critique. Three women scholars – Judith Fetterley, Ann Douglas, and Jane Tompkins – played particularly crucial roles in bringing Stowe back to the forefront of American literary history through complementary, though distinctive, projects.

In 1977, Fetterley and Douglas both brought out books that would exercise enormous influence in American literary studies, including scholarship on Stowe. Fetterley's *The Resisting Reader: A Feminist Approach to American Fiction* presented insistently gendered interpretations of major male authors such as Ernest Hemingway, F. Scott Fitzgerald, and William Faulkner (from the twentieth century), alongside figures such as Nathaniel Hawthorne and Washington Irving (from the nineteenth). Although Fetterley did not in this case take on reclamation of individual women authors, her powerful arguments against their exclusion from the canon established a foundation for recovery work by scholars such as Jane Tompkins. Furthermore, work that Fetterley did later on Stowe, when reevaluating feminist interventions into literary scholarship as an overarching agenda, would both complement and complicate Tompkins's strategies.[29]

Meanwhile, Ann Douglas's *The Feminization of American Culture* proffered a complex blend of celebrating the enormous appeal of Stowe's writing and of critiquing its ideology. Douglas depicted Stowe as achieving mass appeal by encouraging "self-indulgence" in readers, embodying the "sentimental peddling of Christian belief for its nostalgic value," and contributing to the "vitiation and near-disappearance of the Calvinist tradition" of intellectual (i.e., male) rigor. Critical though she was of Stowe and, in particular, of the emblematic character of Little Eva, Douglas took *Uncle Tom's Cabin* quite seriously, and in doing so, brought the author back into play as a figure to be reckoned with in any study of nineteenth-century literary history. By the time Jane Tompkins published *Sensational Designs* in 1985, the groundwork had been laid for a recovery of Stowe as a major figure in American literature. Though she credited Douglas for drawing "critical attention" to the "long-neglected body of work" by authors like Stowe, Tompkins framed her own book as a direct response to Douglas's by casting *The Feminization of American Culture* as both "antisentimentalist" and allied with masculine institutional traditions viewing women's nineteenth-century sentimental literature with "contempt."[30]

Most importantly, in her chapter on *Uncle Tom's Cabin*, Tompkins offered what would become the most influential defense of Stowe to be mounted since the 1850s responses by the novelist's original supporters. Casting her own past tendency to ignore the text as the result of being trained in "the male-dominated scholarly tradition" of American literary history, Tompkins honored the very sentimental strategies that others had regularly denigrated in Stowe's work. Specifically, Tompkins saluted the "evangelical piety and moral commitment" behind novels like *Uncle Tom's Cabin*, whose "popularity," "emotionality," and "religiosity" should be reexamined in positive terms consistent with the values of Stowe's own day. Praising the way that Stowe's first novel sought to "reorganize culture from the woman's point of view," Tompkins asserted that *Uncle Tom's Cabin* should be esteemed for "its intellectual complexity, ambition, and resourcefulness," including a "critique of American society far more devastating than any delivered by better-known critics such as Hawthorne and Melville." For Tompkins, the cultural work of Stowe's novel extended well beyond the domestic sphere so often associated with antebellum women's writing; *Uncle Tom's Cabin*, Tompkins found, had claimed a "mission" that was "global" in scope, having "interests identical with the interests of the race" (Tompkins, *Sensational Designs*, pp. 123–4; 146).

Intriguingly, Tompkins's mention of "the race" in her closing pro-Stowe salvo for *Sensational Designs* seems to have been referencing the *human* race, rather than the category of analysis that would continue to be the basis of much criticism of *Uncle Tom's Cabin* throughout the twentieth century and beyond, even among some women scholars joining Tompkins's campaign to rescue the novel. In that context, scholarship in more recent decades has increasingly grappled with a dimension of Stowe's major book that Tompkins – partly by virtue of her focus on responding to Douglas's "feminization" argument – did not plumb: the troubling racial attitudes inherent in *Uncle Tom's Cabin*'s portrayal of African Americans.

While a number of African American readers had criticized Stowe's portrayal of Tom and her stand on the colonization issue in her own day (see above), the most famous and unrelenting attack on the novel on the grounds of racism was published in the middle of the twentieth century by James Baldwin in the *Partisan Review*. Organizing his critique partly in genre terms, Baldwin decried the inefficacy of the social protest novel form in general, but he targeted *Uncle Tom's Cabin* as the prime offender. Baldwin yoked the text to Louisa May Alcott's *Little Women*, condemning the "ostentatious parading of excessive and spurious emotion" in both novels as signs of "dishonesty, the inability to feel." Asserting that sentimentalism is, in fact, "always . . . the signal of secret and violent inhumanity, the mask of cruelty," Baldwin drew clear distinctions between a true artist (one who can fathom the motivations behind such evils as slavery) and Stowe, merely a propagandist – and one without genuine commitment to the people she claimed to support. For Baldwin, indeed, there is a more pressing charge to mount against Stowe than artistic failures: the "terrible power" of her characterizations, clearly growing out of a persistent racism which has carried over, through the legacies of her text, into later generations of American social life. From Baldwin's perspective, the most honest answer to Stowe's racism is provided in Richard Wright's *Native Son*, a novel written out of bitterness at the role he and his character Bigger Thomas inherited from the lingering influence of blackness as constructed in *Uncle Tom's Cabin*. Hence, for Baldwin, "Bigger is Uncle Tom's descendant, flesh of his flesh, so exactly opposite a portrait that, when the books are placed together, it seems that the contemporary Negro novelist and the dead New England woman are locked together in a deadly, timeless battle; the one uttering merciless exhortations, the other shouting curses."[31]

The charge Baldwin mounted against Stowe has reverberated over the decades since it first appeared, effectively demanding that, despite the necessity of situating her attitudes toward blacks in an informed historical context, we must also acknowledge the negative influence her novel's representations of African Americans continue to exercise. In 1956, the white novelist J. C. Furnas echoed Baldwin's cry against Stowe's legacy in *Goodbye to Uncle Tom*, a book-length inspection of the ways her novel had had a profoundly disturbing effect on American race relations, especially through its contributions to "misconceptions about the American Negro that have plagued the nation ever since" the serial first appeared in the 1850s.[32] Accordingly, though Jane Smiley provocatively asserted in a 1996 essay for *Harper's Magazine* that she would rather her children read *Uncle Tom's Cabin* than Mark Twain's *The Adventures of Huckleberry Finn*, others might point to Smiley's approving attitude as representative of the very problem Baldwin had so forcefully identified.

In that regard, we should note how Smiley's *Harper's* essay anchors her praise of *Uncle Tom's Cabin* and Stowe in the character of little Eva – the figure so closely linked to sentimental white sympathy, though with quite different valuations, both in Baldwin's critique and in 1970s and 1980s feminist scholarship. Smiley argues that Stowe's novel should be recognized as "'great' literature" because of its high purpose and straightforward portrayals of slavery's ills, with "no whitewash."[33] However, as Baldwin and others have reminded us, reading through the perspective of Eva – reading through whites' tears – does, after all, create a kind of "whitewash" of slavery, promoting an inability to recognize fully and resist forcefully the racism at its core.

To enact an informed cultural critique of Stowe that takes into account such complex legacies as her characters' residual influence on race relations, scholarship has been placing increasing emphasis on cultural studies that position not just the author but also particular readers and comparative analysis in specific historical contexts. Robert Levine, for instance, has explored the responses to *Uncle Tom's Cabin* and Stowe as recorded in *Frederick Douglass' Paper* over many months' time in the 1850s; Elizabeth Young has examined *Uncle Tom's Cabin* as part of a larger body of women's writing about the Civil

War, including familiar texts by well-known authors such as Louisa May Alcott and Margaret Mitchell, but also lesser-known ones such as memoirs by Elizabeth Keckley (White House seamstress to Mary Todd Lincoln) and Loreta Velazquez, who masqueraded as a Confederate soldier.[34] In James Olney's discussion of recordings by singer Mae Barnes, we see a playful but determined assault on Uncle Tom-associated traditions – a reading of the novel whereby both Barnes and Olney can take Stowe to task, while simultaneously affirming the novel's inescapable impact. Olney focuses on two songs by Barnes: "I Ain't Gonna Be No Topsy" and "Paris Is My Old Kentucky Home." Through an historically sensitive close reading of the lyrics, Olney shows how Barnes's music marshals humor to temper angry bitterness, thus *performing* an identity resisting the stereotypes that Stowe's novel and its textual heirs have produced.[35] Furthermore, in an anecdote describing his experience playing a scratchy old record of Barnes's singing for James Baldwin himself to hear, Olney links his own scholarship with a tradition of African Americans' artistic resistance to the cultural capital Stowe still wields.

New directions in Stowe studies

Research on Harriet Beecher Stowe has entered a new era in the twenty-first century, and not based solely on chronology. Studies of Stowe's authorship now extend beyond *Uncle Tom's Cabin* to other works, particularly their contributions to literary movements such as regionalism, social satire, and travel writing.

Building on the work that reestablished Stowe as a central figure in American literature, scholars are now positioning her career in a transnational context. These efforts to internationalize Stowe studies are exploring how her career was shaped by reading, meeting, and corresponding with European contemporaries, such as George Eliot, Lady Byron, and Harriet Martineau – not to mention the uses she made of such youthful favorites as Sir Walter Scott and Shakespeare. Comparative studies of Stowe's writing are also on the rise, placing her in productive dialogue with authors ranging from Eugène Sue, on the one hand, to Caribbean American writers like José Martí and Pierre Faubert, on the other.[36]

Another important trend is situating Stowe in popular culture studies. For example, Robyn Warhol has traced themes and characters from *Uncle Tom's Cabin* in a wide array of playbills. In broader terms, Jim O'Loughlin has pointed to the "coordinating role" that *Uncle Tom's Cabin* (both as a progressive and as a reactionary text) has played in the American culture industry.[37]

Like the scholarship on Stowe's works, biographical analysis has also flourished. The rearticulation of Stowe's importance to American and European literary history in the 1970s and 1980s encouraged reexaminations of her personal history as well. Joan Hedrick's Pulitzer-prize-winning *Harriet Beecher Stowe: A Life* marked a turning point. While drawing extensively on previous treatments of Stowe – such as Annie Fields's sympathetic portrait and the account by son Charles Stowe – Hedrick's 1990s study incorporated new archival resources into her study of Stowe. Furthermore, informed by the developments in women's studies since the time of Forrest Wilson's earlier Pulitzer-prize-winner, *Crusader in Crinoline*, Hedrick's biography benefited from an expanded theoretical grounding.[38] Hedrick's book, in turn, supported more biographical analyses, such as Barbara A. White's *The Beecher Sisters* and Samuel A. Schreiner, Jr.'s *The Passionate Beechers*.[39] Emphasizing connections between Stowe's career choices and her affiliation with the Beecher clan, these latter two books exemplify the degree to which Harriet Beecher Stowe and her extended family have reclaimed a significant place in American history.

Finally, perhaps there is no stronger indicator of the enhanced position Stowe now holds in the international literary marketplace today than the escalating number of paperback editions of her writing, particularly, of course, *Uncle Tom's Cabin*. Though most of these target university students, some are pitched to general readers and high school classrooms – an indicator that Stowe may be reestablishing herself as an author with multiple audiences. One striking benchmark of Stowe's re-canonization was the *Norton Critical Edition* that Elizabeth Ammons published for *Uncle Tom's Cabin* in 1994. As an example of the internationalization of Stowe as an academic subject, we need only point to the Oxford World's Classics paperback edited by Jean Fagan Yellin, which marks the increasing attention being given to race issues by including in its appendix Frederick Douglass's "The Heroic Slave," along with excerpts from *A Key to Uncle Tom's Cabin*.[40]

For general (if serious-minded) readers, as well as students, the Modern Library recruited Jane Smiley to follow up on her appreciative *Harper's Magazine* essay touting Stowe over Twain by writing an introduction to one recent edition, which also provides discussion questions for reading groups. In describing Stowe's novel as "compelling, readable, wise, and well-constructed," Smiley's introduction proposes that *Uncle Tom's Cabin* "ought to be required reading in every high school in America," and endorses the book as "the most important American literary document of the nineteenth century."[41] If *Uncle Tom's Cabin* is no longer literally a book for the millions, the novel and its author have certainly reasserted a claim to popular culture as well as academic significance.

African American novelist Charles Johnson's introductory treatment of Stowe and her novel in a 150th-anniversary edition of *Uncle Tom's Cabin* is telling in this regard. Johnson describes Stowe's "most thoroughly American" book as "a cultural artifact; a Rosetta stone for black images in American fiction, theater, and film," as well as "the Urtext or common coin for discussions about slavery." As such, Johnson says, *Uncle Tom's Cabin* offers "an interpretation that we may love or hate, admire or despise, defend or reject, in whole or in part. It is nonetheless a story that so permeates white popular and literary culture, and sits so high astride nineteenth-century American fiction, that it simply can never be ignored."[42]

Notes

1 Life

1. Charles Edward Stowe, *Life of Harriet Beecher Stowe, Compiled from Her Letters and Journals* (Boston: Houghton, Mifflin and Company: 1889), p. 154.
2. Florine Thayer McCray, *The Life and Work of Harriet Beecher Stowe* (Honolulu: University Press of the Pacific, 2004; repr. of 1889), p. 440.
3. Annie Fields, *Life and Letters of Harriet Beecher Stowe* (Honolulu: University Press of the Pacific, 2003; repr. 1897), pp. preface, 268–9.
4. Joseph A. Conforti, *Imagining New England: Explorations of Regional Identity from the Pilgrims to the Twentieth Century* (Chapel Hill: University of North Carolina Press, 2001), pp. 3, 13, 12.
5. Catharine Beecher, *Educational Reminiscences and Suggestions* (New York: J. B. Ford, 1874).
6. *Catalogue of the Officers, Teachers, and Pupils of the Hartford Female Seminary for the Summer Term of 1828.* Hartford Female Seminary Catalogue. Folder 320, Beecher-Stowe Family Papers. Schlesinger Library, Radcliffe Institute, Harvard University.
7. Catharine Beecher, *Suggestions Respecting Improvements in Education* (Hartford: Packard & Butler, 1829).
8. *The Semicolon* (Cincinnati: E. Morgan and Company, 1845).
9. Mary Louise Pratt, *Imperial Eyes: Travel Writing and Transculturation* (New York: Routledge, 1992).
10. Joan D. Hedrick, *Harriet Beecher Stowe: A Life* (New York: Oxford University Press, 1994), p. 194.
11. Harriet Beecher Stowe to Sarah Josepha Hale, November 10, 1851, HM24166. The Huntington Library, San Marino, Calif.
12. Charles Beecher, *Harriet Beecher Stowe in Europe: The Journal of Charles Beecher*, eds. Joseph S. Van Why and Earl French (Hartford: Stowe-Day Foundation, 1986), pp. 57–8.
13. Qtd in Mary B. Graff and Edith Cowles, "The Author," *Palmetto Leaves* by Harriet Beecher Stowe (Gainesville: University Press of Florida, 1999; facsimile repr. Boston: J. F. Osgood, 1873), p. x.

2 Cultural contexts

1. Sarah Robbins, *Managing Literacy, Mothering America: Women's Narratives on Reading and Writing in the Nineteenth Century* (Pittsburgh: University of Pittsburgh Press, 2004), pp. 20–30.
2. Robbins, *Managing Literacy*, pp. 93–109.
3. [Sydney Smith], Review on *Statistical Annals of the United States of America* by Adam Seybert, *Edinburgh Review* 33 (1820), 69–80.
4. "Editorial Notes: American Literature and Reprints," *Putnam's Magazine* (November 1855), 543–5.
5. Cathy N. Davidson, *Revolution and the Word: The Rise of the Novel in America* (New York: Oxford University Press, 1986); Nina Baym, *Woman's Fiction: A Guide to Novels by and about Women in America 1820–1870*. 2nd edition (Urbana: University of Illinois Press, 1993).
6. Michael Denning, *Mechanic Accents: Dime Novels and Working Class Culture in America* (New York: Verso, 1998), pp. 10–13.
7. Jacqueline Jones, *American Work: Four Centuries of Black and White Labor* (New York: W. W. Norton, 1998), p. 248.
8. Samuel A. Schreiner, Jr., *The Passionate Beechers: A Family Saga of Sanctity and Scandal That Changed America* (New York: John Wiley and Sons, 2003).
9. Lyman Abbott, *Henry Ward Beecher* (New York: Chelsea House, 1980).
10. Joan D. Hedrick, "'Peaceable Fruits': The Ministry of Harriet Beecher Stowe," *American Quarterly* 40 (1988), 307–32.
11. Louise L. Stevenson, *The Victorian Homefront: American Thought and Culture, 1860–1880* (New York: Twayne, 1991); Stow Persons, *The Decline of American Gentility* (New York: Columbia University Press, 1973), p. 26; Steven Mintz, *A Prison of Expectations: The Family in Victorian Culture* (New York: New York University Press, 1983), pp. 8, 29, 195, 206.

3 Works

1. Harriet Beecher Stowe, "Uncle Lot," in *American Women Regionalists: A Norton Anthology*, eds. Judith Fetterley and Marjorie Pryse (New York: W. W. Norton, 1992), p. 4.
2. Sandra A. Zagarell, "'America' as Community in Three Antebellum Village Sketches," in *The (Other) American Traditions: Nineteenth-Century Women Writers*, ed. Joyce W. Warren (New Brunswick: Rutgers University Press, 1993), p. 144.
3. Harriet Beecher Stowe, "Introductory Note," in *Stories, Sketches and Studies* (Cambridge: Riverside Press, 1896), pp. vii–viii.
4. Sarah Robbins, "Gendering the History of the Anti-slavery Narrative: Juxtaposing *Uncle Tom's Cabin* and *Benito Cereno, Beloved* and *Middle Passage*," *American Quarterly* 49 (1997), 537.

5. Qtd in Barbara Hochman, "*Uncle Tom's Cabin* in the *National Era*: An Essay in Generic Norms and the Contexts of Reading," in *Book History*, eds. Ezra Greenspan and Jonathan Ross, 7 (2004), p. 145.
6. Qtd in Claire Parfait, "The Nineteenth-Century Serial as a Collective Enterprise: Harriet Beecher Stowe's *Uncle Tom's Cabin* and Eugene Sue's *Les Mystères de Paris*," *Proceedings of the American Antiquarian Society* 112 (2002), 137.
7. Susan Belasco Smith, "Serialization and the Nature of *Uncle Tom's Cabin*," in *Periodical Literature in Nineteenth-Century America*, eds. Kenneth M. Price and Susan Belasco Smith (Charlottesville: University Press of Virginia, 1995), pp. 69–89.
8. Michael Winship, "'The Greatest Book of Its Kind': A Publishing History of 'Uncle Tom's Cabin,'" *Proceedings of the American Antiquarian Society* 109 (1999), 313.
9. Thomas F. Gossett, '*Uncle Tom's Cabin*' *and American Culture* (Dallas: Southern Methodist University Press, 1985), p. 91.
10. Ann Douglas, *The Feminization of American Culture* (New York: Anchor Books/Doubleday, 1977), p. 97.
11. Harriet Beecher Stowe, *Uncle Tom's Cabin or, Life Among the Lowly*, ed. Ann Douglas (New York, Penguin, 1981), p. 233.
12. Cynthia Griffin Wolff, "'Masculinity' in *Uncle Tom's Cabin*," *American Quarterly* 47 (1995), 599, 602, 601, 603.
13. Ronald Takaki, "The Metaphysics of Civilization: 'The Black Race Within Our Bosom,'" in *Iron Cages: Race and Culture in Nineteenth-Century America* (New York: Oxford University Press, 2000), pp. 108–44.
14. Timothy B. Powell, *Ruthless Democracy: A Multicultural Interpretation of the American Renaissance* (Princeton: Princeton University Press, 2000), pp. 111–12.
15. Powell, *Ruthless*, pp. 115–23.
16. Susan M. Ryan, "Charity Begins at Home: Stowe's Anti-slavery Novels and the Forms of Benevolent Citizenship," *American Literature* 72 (2000), 762.
17. Arthur Riss, "Racial Essentialism and Family Values in *Uncle Tom's Cabin*," *American Quarterly* 46 (1994), 517.
18. Linda Williams, *Playing the Race Card: Melodramas of Black and White from Uncle Tom to O. J. Simpson* (Princeton: Princeton University Press, 2001), pp. 65–77.
19. Eric Lott, *Love and Theft: Blackface Minstrelsy and the American Working Class* (New York: Oxford University Press, 1993), pp. 15, 8, 17.
20. Sarah Meer, *Uncle Tom Mania: Slavery, Minstrelsy, and Transatlantic Culture in the 1850s* (Athens: University of Georgia Press, 2005), p. 12.
21. Charles Chesnutt, *The Conjure Woman* (Boston: Houghton Mifflin, 1899).
22. Joseph Boskin, *Sambo: The Rise and Demise of an American Jester* (New York: Oxford University Press, 1986), pp. 16 and 5.
23. Jane Tompkins, *Sensational Designs: The Cultural Work of American Fiction, 1790–1860* (New York: Oxford University Press, 1985), p. 127.
24. Marianne Noble, *The Masochistic Pleasures of Sentimental Literature* (Princeton: Princeton University Press, 2000); Karen Sanchez-Eppler, *Touching Liberty:*

Abolition, Feminism, and the Politics of the Body (Berkeley: University of California Press, 1997).

25. Lori Merish, *Sentimental Materialism: Gender, Commodity Culture, and Nineteenth-Century American Literature* (Durham: Duke University Press, 2000), p. 139.

26. Elizabeth Ammons, "Stowe's Dream of the Mother-Savior: *Uncle Tom's Cabin* and American Women Writers before the 1920s," in *New Essays on Stowe's "Uncle Tom's Cabin,"* ed. Eric J. Sundquist (Cambridge: Cambridge University Press, 1986), pp. 155–95; Gillian Brown, *Domestic Individualism: Imagining Self in Nineteenth-Century America* (Berkeley: University of California Press, 1990), pp. 13–38; Lora Romero, "Bio-political Resistance: Harriet Beecher Stowe," in *Home Fronts: Domesticity and its Critics in the Antebellum United States* (Durham: Duke University Press, 1997), pp. 70–88.

27. Uncle Tom's Cabin in American Culture, http://www.iath.virginia.edu/utc/uncletom/illustra/ilhp.html.

28. Harriet Beecher Stowe, *A Key to Uncle Tom's Cabin* (Boston: John P. Jewett, 1853; reprint, Bedford: Applewood Books, 1970), p. 17.

29. Richard H. Brodhead, "Sparing the Rod: Discipline and Fiction in Antebellum America," in *Cultures of Letters: Scenes of Reading and Writing in Nineteenth-Century America* (Chicago: University of Chicago Press, 1993), pp. 13–47.

30. Hedrick, *Harriet Beecher Stowe*, p. 221; Winship, "Publishing History," 317–18.

31. Charles Stowe, *Life*, p. 160; Debra J. Rosenthal, *A Routledge Literary Sourcebook on Harriet Beecher Stowe's "Uncle Tom's Cabin"* (New York: Routledge, 2004), p. 29.

32. Winship, "History," 322.

33. Melissa J. Homestead, "'When I Can Read My Title Clear': Harriet Beecher Stowe and the *Stowe v. Thomas* Copyright Infringement Case (1853)," in *American Women Authors and Literary Property, 1822–1869* (Cambridge: Cambridge University Press, 2005), pp. 105–49.

34. Cindy Weinstein, "*Uncle Tom's Cabin* and the South" in *The Cambridge Companion to Harriet Beecher Stowe*, ed. Cindy Weinstein (Cambridge: Cambridge University Press, 2004), p. 50.

35. Ronald G. Walters, "Stowe and the American Reform Tradition," in Weinstein, *Cambridge Companion to Harriet Beecher Stowe*, p. 181.

36. Jeannine Marie DeLombard, "Representing the Slave: White Advocacy and Black Testimony in Harriet Beecher Stowe's *Dred*," *The New England Quarterly* 75 (2002), 84.

37. Harriet Beecher Stowe, *Dred: A Tale of the Great Dismal Swamp*, ed. Robert S. Levine (Phillips, Sampson and Company, 1856; reprint, New York, Penguin, 2000), p. 167.

38. Judie Newman, "Staging Black Insurrection: *Dred* on Stage," in Weinstein, *Cambridge Companion to Harriet Beecher Stowe*, 113–30.

39. Lawrence Buell, "The Dream of the Great American Novel," in Weinstein, *Cambridge Companion to Harriet Beecher Stowe*, 193; 196–200.

40. Gossett, "*Uncle Tom's Cabin*" *and American Culture*, p. 261.

41. Qtd in Gossett, ibid, p. 266.

42. Eric Gardner, "Stowe Takes the Stage: Harriet Beecher Stowe's *The Christian Slave*," *Legacy* 15 (1998), 79.

43. Michelle Wallace, "The Celluloid Cabin: Satirical Distortions of Uncle Tom in Animated Cartoon Shorts, 1932–1947," *Popular Culture* 23 (2001), 1–2.

44. Robyn R. Warhol, "'Ain't I De One Everybody Come to See?!': Popular Culture Memories of *Uncle Tom's Cabin*," in *Hop on Pop: The Politics and Pleasures of Popular Culture*, eds. Henry Jenkins, Tara McPherson, and Jane Shattuc (Durham: Duke University Press, 2002), p. 653.

45. Robert Alexander, *I Ain't Yo' Uncle: The New Jack Revisionist "Uncle Tom's Cabin"* (Woodstock: Dramatic Publishing, 1996), pp. 6, 9, 7.

46. Mary Suzanne Schriber, *Writing Home: American Women Abroad, 1830–1920* (Charlottesville: University Press of Virginia, 1997), pp. 7–10.

47. Harriet Beecher Stowe, *Sunny Memories of Foreign Lands* (Boston: Phillips, Sampson, and Company, 1854), 1: preface.

48. Harriet Beecher Stowe, *Agnes of Sorrento* (St Clair Shores: Scholarly Press, 1970; reprint of Boston: Houghton Mifflin, 1890), p. vi.

49. Gail K. Smith, "Art and the Body in *Agnes of Sorrento*," in *Transatlantic Stowe: Essays on Harriet Beecher Stowe and European Culture*, eds. Emily Todd, Sarah Meer, and Denise Kohn (Iowa City: University of Iowa Press, 2006), manuscript copy.

50. Annamaria Formichella, "Domesticity and Nationalism in Harriet Beecher Stowe's *Agnes of Sorrento*," *Legacy* 15 (1998), 195.

51. Harriet Beecher Stowe, *Palmetto Leaves*, eds. Mary B. Graff and Edith Cowles (Gainesville, University Press of Florida, 1999; reprint of Boston: James R. Osgood, 1873), p. 35.

52. Marjorie Pryse, "Stowe and Regionalism," in Weinstein, *Cambridge Companion to Harriet Beecher Stowe*, pp. 134, 131.

53. Conforti, *Imagining New England*, pp. 96, 144–5.

54. Joan D. Hedrick, "Foreword" to *The Pearl of Orr's Island: A Story of the Coast of Maine* by Harriet Beecher Stowe (Boston: Houghton Mifflin, 2001; reprint of 1862), pp. xii–xiii.

55. Gillian Brown, "Reading and Children," in Weinstein, *Cambridge Companion to Harriet Beecher Stowe*, p. 89; Marjorie Pryse, "Stowe and Regionalism," in Weinstein, *Cambridge Companion to Harriet Beecher Stowe*, pp. 137–9; Judith Fetterley, "Only a Story, Not a Romance": Harriet Beecher Stowe's *The Pearl of Orr's Island*, in Warren, *The (Other) American Traditions*, pp. 108–25.

56. Susan K. Harris, "Introduction" to *The Minister's Wooing* by Harriet Beecher Stowe (New York: Penguin Classics, 1999), p. viii.

57. Dorothy Berkson, "Introduction" to *Oldtown Folks* by Harriet Beecher Stowe (New Brunswick: Rutgers University Press, 1987), pp. xxxvi and xxiii.

58. Qtd in Edward Tang, "Making Declarations of Her Own: Harriet Beecher Stowe as New England Historian," *The New England Quarterly* 71 (1998), 86; from Bret Harte, "Culture and Christianity," *Scribner's Monthly* (July 1878): 432.

59. Ellery Sedgwick, *The Atlantic Monthly 1857–1909: Yankee Humanism at High Tide and Ebb* (Amherst: University of Massachusetts Press, 1994), p. 86.
60. Sarah Robbins, "Gendering Gilded Age Periodical Professionalism: Reading Harriet Beecher Stowe's *Hearth and Home* Prescriptions for Women's Writing," in *"The Only Efficient Instrument": American Women Writers and the Periodical, 1837–1916*, eds. Aleta Cane and Susan Alves (Iowa City: University of Iowa Press, 2001), pp. 45–65.
61. Harriet Beecher Stowe, "The True Story of Lady Byron's Life," in *The Oxford Harriet Beecher Stowe Reader*, ed. Joan D. Hedrick (New York: Oxford University Press, 1999), pp. 553, 557.
62. Greg Crane, "Stowe and the Law," in Weinstein, *Cambridge Companion to Harriet Beecher Stowe*, p. 167.
63. Carolyn Karcher, "Stowe and the Literature of Social Change," in Weinstein, *Cambridge Companion to Harriet Beecher Stowe*, p. 204.
64. Harriet Beecher Stowe, *Pink and White Tyranny: A Society Novel* (New York: Plume, 1988; reprint of Boston: Roberts Brothers, 1871), p. vi.
65. Qtd in Kathleen De Grave, "Introduction," *The Jungle: The Uncensored Original Edition* by Upton Sinclair (Tucson: See Sharp Press, 2003), p. xviii.
66. De Grave, p. xviii; Upton Sinclair, *The Jungle: The Uncensored Original Edition* (Tucson: See Sharp Press, 2003), back cover.
67. "Insider Q and A: Scott Turow," *TV Guide* (23 May 2004), 12.

4 Reception and critics

1. Nina Baym, *Novels, Readers and Reviewers: Responses to Fiction in Antebellum America* (Ithaca: Cornell University Press, 1984); Dan Brown, *The Da Vinci Code* (New York: Doubleday, 2003).
2. Elizabeth Moss, *Domestic Novelists in the Old South: Defenders of Southern Culture* (Baton Rouge: Louisiana State University Press, 1992), pp. 101–2.
3. Gossett, *"Uncle Tom's Cabin" and American Culture*, pp. 185, 189–90.
4. Charles F. Briggs, "Uncle Tomitudes," *Putnam's Monthly Magazine* (January 1853), 97–102; excerpt reprinted in *A Routledge Literary Sourcebook on Harriet Beecher Stowe's "Uncle Tom's Cabin,"* ed. Debra J. Rosenthal (New York: Routledge, 2004), p. 32.
5. Mary H. Eastman, *Aunt Phillis's Cabin; or, Southern Life as It Is* (Philadelphia: Lippincott, Grambo and Company, 1852); J. Thornton Randolph, *The Cabin and the Parlor; or, Slaves and Masters* (Philadelphia: T. B. Peterson, 1852); William J. Grayson. *The Hireling and the Slave, Chicora and Other Poems* (Charleston, SC: McCarter and Company, 1856).
6. Robert Criswell, *"Uncle Tom's Cabin" Contrasted with Buckingham Hall, the Planter's Home* (New York: D. Fanshaw, 1852), p. 7.
7. Annie Jefferson Holland, *The Refugees: A Sequel to "Uncle Tom's Cabin."* (Austin: Published for the Author, 1892), pp. 6–8.

8. Williams, *Race Card*, pp. 101–35.
9. F. C. Adams, *Uncle Tom at Home: A Review of the Reviewers and Repudiators of Uncle Tom's Cabin by Mrs. Stowe* (New York: Books for Libraries Press, 1970; repr., 1853), pp. v, 42–3, 48–50, 99, 8–9.
10. Marva Banks, "*Uncle Tom's Cabin* and Antebellum Black Response," in *Readers in History: Nineteenth-Century American Literature and the Contexts of Response*, ed. James L. Machor (Baltimore: Johns Hopkins University Press), pp. 212–13.
11. Banks, "*Uncle Tom's Cabin* and Antebellum," pp. 220–4; Gossett, "*Uncle Tom's Cobin*" *and American Culture*, pp. 173–4.
12. Toni Morrison, *Playing in the Dark: Whiteness and the Literary Imagination* (New York: Vintage Books, 1992), pp. 16–17.
13. Robert B. Stepto, "Sharing the Thunder: The Literary Exchanges of Harriet Beecher Stowe, Henry Bibb, and Frederick Douglass," in *New Essays on "Uncle Tom's Cabin,"* ed. Eric J. Sundquist (Cambridge: Cambridge University Press, 1986), p. 150.
14. Peter A. Dorsey, "De-Authorizing Slavery: Realism in Stowe's *Uncle Tom's Cabin* and Brown's *Clotel*," *ESQ* 41 (1995), 256–88.
15. Ishmael Reed, *Flight to Canada* (New York: Random House, 1976), p. 8, italics in original.
16. William Wells Brown, *Clotel; or, The President's Daughter: A Narrative of Slave Life in the United States. With a Sketch of the Author's Life* (New York: Carol Publishing, 1969; repr., London: Partridge & Oakey, 1853), p. 52.
17. Harriet Jacobs to [Amy Post], Cornwall [New York], February 1853, in Jean Fagan Yellin, *Harriet Jacobs: A Life* (New York: Basic Books, 2004), p. 120; Jacobs qtd. in Yellin, *ibid.*, p. 121; Jacobs to Post, in Yellin, p. 124.
18. Frances Smith Foster, "Introduction," *A Brighter Coming Day: A Frances Ellen Watkins Harper Reader* (New York: City University of New York), p. 11.
19. Richard Yarborough, "Strategies of Black Characterization in *Uncle Tom's Cabin* and the Early Afro-American Novel," in Sundquist, *New Essays on* UTC, pp. 45–84.
20. A. Philip Randolph, "Pullman Porters Need Own Union," *Frederick Douglass' Paper* 7 (1925), 290.
21. Richard Wright, *Uncle Tom's Children* (New York: Perennial/Harper Collins, 1991; reprint of, 1940), p. xxxi.
22. Morrison, *Playing in the Dark*, p. 52.
23. Houston A. Baker, *Turning South Again: Re-thinking Modernism/Re-reading Booker T.* (Durham: Duke University Press, 2001), pp. 16–17, 27–28, 44–45, 2.
24. James Baldwin, *Notes of a Native Son* (Boston: Beacon Press, 1955; repr., 1984), p. 3.
25. George Sand, "Review of *Uncle Tom's Cabin*," *La Presse* (December 17, 1852), reprinted in Fields, *Life and Letters*, pp. 151–2.
26. Meer, *Uncle Tom Mania*, pp. 134, 2; Gossett, "*Uncle Tom's Cabin*" *and American Culture*, p. 239.
27. Jan Marsh, "From Slave Cabin to Windsor Castle: Josiah Henson and 'Uncle Tom' in Britain," *Nineteenth-Century Studies* 16 (2002), 46.

28. Eric J. Sundquist, "Introduction," in Sundquist, *New Essays on "Uncle Tom's Cabin,"* pp. 2–3.
29. Judith Fetterley, *The Resisting Reader: A Feminist Approach to American Fiction* (Bloomington: Indiana University Press, 1978); Fetterley, "Commentary: Nineteenth-Century American Women Writers and the Politics of Recovery," *American Literary History* 6 (1994), 600–11.
30. Douglas, *Feminization*, pp. 4, 6, 7; Tompkins, *Sensational Designs*, p. 217 n. 3.
31. James Baldwin, "Everybody's Protest Novel," reprint of the 1949 essay in *Partisan Review, Notes of a Native Son* (Boston: Beacon Press, 1955; repr., 1983), pp. 14, 16, 22.
32. J. C. Furnas, *Goodbye to Uncle Tom* (New York: William Sloane, 1956), back flap.
33. Jane Smiley, "Say It Ain't So, Huck: Second Thoughts on Mark Twain's 'masterpiece,'" *Harper's Magazine* 292 (1996), 67.
34. Robert S. Levine, "*Uncle Tom's Cabin* in *Frederick Douglass' Paper*: An Analysis of Reception," *American Literature* 64 (1992), 71–93; Elizabeth Young, *Disarming the Nation: Women's Writing and the American Civil War* (Chicago: University of Chicago Press, 1999).
35. James Olney, "'I Ain't Gonna Be No Topsy' Because 'Paris Is My Old Kentucky Home,'" *The Southern Review* 37 (2001), 155–67.
36. Parfait, "The Nineteenth-Century Serial," 137; Anna Brickhouse, "The Writing of Haiti: Pierre Faubert, Harriet Beecher Stowe, and Beyond, *American Literary History* 13 (2001), 407–44.
37. Warhol, "Ain't I De One," pp. 650–70; Jim O'Loughlin, "Articulating *Uncle Tom's Cabin*," *New Literary History* 31 (2000), 574.
38. Forrest Wilson, *Crusader in Crinoline: The Life of Harriet Beecher Stowe* (Westport: Greenwood Press, 1941).
39. Barbara A. White, *The Beecher Sisters* (New Haven: Yale University Press, 2003); Schreiner, *Passionate Beechers*.
40. Harriet Beecher Stowe, *Uncle Tom's Cabin*, ed. Jean Fagan Yellin (New York: Oxford University Press, 1998).
41. Jane Smiley, "Introduction," *Uncle Tom's Cabin* by Harriet Beecher Stowe (New York: Modern Library, 2001), p. xiii.
42. Charles Johnson, "Introduction," *Uncle Tom's Cabin* by Harriet Beecher Stowe (Oxford: Oxford University Press, 2002), p. v.

Further reading

Editions

See the discussion of editions of *Uncle Tom's Cabin* in the "Reception" chapter. Citations appearing in earlier chapters of this book come from this paperback edition: *Uncle Tom's Cabin or, Life Among the Lowly*, edited with an introduction by Ann Douglas (New York: Penguin, 1986). Two other paperback editions provide especially helpful contextual materials: *Uncle Tom's Cabin, a Norton Critical Edition*, edited by Elizabeth Ammons (New York: W.W. Norton, 1994); and *Uncle Tom's Cabin*, edited by Jean Fagan Yellin (Oxford: Oxford University Press, 1998). Another useful edition includes samples of Stowe's early writing and sketches about home-making, as well as *Uncle Tom's Cabin* and other anti-slavery texts, in a single volume: *The Oxford Harriet Beecher Stowe Reader*, edited with an introduction by Joan D. Hedrick (Oxford: Oxford University Press, 1999).

Listed below are accessible editions of additional works which are receiving increased attention from scholars:

Agnes of Sorrento (St Clair Shores: Scholarly Press, 1970; reprint of Boston: Houghton, Mifflin and Company, 1890)

The American Woman's Home [with Catharine E. Beecher], edited by Nicole Tonkovich (Hartford: Harriet Beecher Stowe Center, 2002)

Dred: A Tale of the Great Dismal Swamp, edited with an introduction by Robert S. Levine (New York: Penguin, 2000)

House and Home Papers (Whitefish: Kessinger Publishing, 2003)

A Key to Uncle Tom's Cabin (Bedford: Applewood, 1970; reprint of Boston: John P. Jewett, 1853)

The Minister's Wooing, edited with an introduction by Susan K. Harris (New York: Penguin, 1999)

Oldtown Folks, edited by Dorothy Berkson (New Brunswick: Rutgers University Press, 1987)

Palmetto Leaves, edited with introductions by Mary B. Graff and Edith Cowles (Gainesville: University Press of Florida, 1999; reprint of Boston: J. F. Osgood, 1873)

The Pearl of Orr's Island: A Story of the Cost of Maine, with a foreword by Joan D. Hedrick (Boston: Houghton Mifflin, 2001)

Pink and White Tyranny: A Society Novel (New York, Plume, 1988); or (Ann Arbor: Michigan Historical Reprint Series, 2005)

Selected biographies

Annie Fields, editor, *Life and Letters of Harriet Beecher Stowe* (Honolulu: University Press of the Pacific, 2003; reprint 1897)
  • Portrait of Stowe by one of her close friends
Joan D. Hedrick, *Harriet Beecher Stowe: A Life* (Oxford: Oxford University Press, 1994)
  • Reshapes Stowe's biography while revising material from earlier treatments, such as Forrest Wilson's *Crusader in Crinoline* (1941); draws from extensive archival research
Samuel A. Schreiner, Jr, *The Passionate Beechers: A Family Saga of Sanctity and Scandal that Changed America* (Hoboken: John Wiley and Sons, 2003)
  • Lays out a group biography of the Beechers as one of the most influential families in nineteenth-century American history; connects Stowe's work as an author with the political and religious leadership being exercised by her brothers and sisters
Charles Edward Stowe, *Life of Harriet Beecher Stowe* (Boston: Houghton, Mifflin and Company, 1889)
  • Reminisces about Stowe's life from the perspective of her son
Barbara A. White, *The Beecher Sisters* (New Haven: Yale University Press, 2003)
  • Chronicles the careers of Catharine, Harriet, and Isabella Beecher and their impact on American education, literature, and the women's movement

Criticism and responses

Robert Alexander, *I Ain't Yo' Uncle: The New Jack Revisionist "Uncle Tom's Cabin"* (Woodstock: Dramatic Publishing, 1996)
  • Challenges the heritage of *Uncle Tom's Cabin* by re-writing the narrative as a performance text reflecting blacks' critiques of Stowe
James Baldwin, *Notes of a Native Son* (Boston: Beacon Press, 1955. Reprint, 1984)
  • Reprints Baldwin's famous assault on *Uncle Tom's Cabin* – "Everybody's Protest Novel" – originally published in 1949
Marva Banks, "Uncle Tom's Cabin and Antebellum Black Response," in *Readers in History: Nineteenth-Century American Literature and the Contexts of Response*, edited by James L. Machor (Baltimore: Johns Hopkins University Press, 1993), pp. 209–27.
  • Describes northern African Americans' reactions to *Uncle Tom's Cabin* in the years just after its publication, while noting strategies leaders used to respond to the text

Nina Baym, *Woman's Fiction: A Guide to Novels by and About Women in America 1820–1870.* 2nd edition (Urbana: University of Illinois Press, 1993)
  • Positions *Uncle Tom's Cabin* as, in some ways, atypical for women's antebellum writing; presents readings of several late-career novels by Stowe

Joseph A. Conforti, *Imagining New England: Explorations of Regional Identity from the Pilgrims to the Mid-Twentieth Century* (Chapel Hill: University of North Carolina Press, 2001)
  • Describes the "national region" of New England as a space and vision negotiated over time through a range of cultural practices; analyzes how Stowe's writing contributes to this agenda

Ann Douglas, *The Feminization of American Culture* (New York: Anchor/ Doubleday, 1977)
  • Traces the formation of an alliance between the nineteenth-century male clergy and educated women, who, Douglas argues, fostered sentimental values in American culture; includes discussion of key Stowe texts

J. C. Furnas, *Goodbye to Uncle Tom* (New York: William Sloane Associates, 1956)
  • Presents a white novelist's forceful critique of *Uncle Tom's Cabin* as having negative impact on American race relations

Thomas F. Gossett, *Uncle Tom's Cabin and American Culture* (Dallas: Southern Methodist University Press, 1985)
  • Traces Stowe's biography and the wide range of responses to *Uncle Tom's Cabin*, with emphasis on ways the novel influenced American culture

Melissa J. Homestead, "'When I Can Read My Title Clear': Harriet Beecher Stowe and the *Stowe v. Thomas* Copyright Infringement Case (1853)," in *American Women Authors and Literary Property, 1822–1869* (Cambridge: Cambridge University Press, 2005), pp. 105–49
  • Examines the legal case through which Stowe attempted (but failed) to exercise copyright control over her novel in the days before strong intellectual property traditions had been established in the US

Mary Kelley, *Private Woman, Public Stage: Literary Domesticity in Nineteenth-Century America* (New York: Oxford University Press, 1984)
  • Develops the category of "literary domestics" for studying works by Stowe and other women writers; connects issues of gender and power to historical trends in the literary marketplace

Denise Kohn, Sarah Meer, and Emily B. Todd, eds., *Transatlantic Stowe: Harriet Beecher Stowe and European Culture* (Iowa City: University of Iowa Press, 2006)
  • Reads Stowe's career as central to nineteenth-century literary culture in America and in Europe; written by scholars in the United States, England, Ireland, and Wales, focuses on issues surrounding national identity, race, class, labor, and the figure of Stowe as a transnational writer

Sarah Meer, *Uncle Tom Mania: Slavery, Minstrelsy, and Transatlantic Culture in the 1850s* (Athens: University of Georgia Press, 2005)
- Examines *Uncle Tom's Cabin* as a transatlantic phenomenon linked to popular culture's fascination with minstrelsy and consumers' desire for material goods

Elizabeth Moss, *Domestic Novels in the Old South: Defenders of Southern Culture* (Baton Rouge: Louisiana State University Press, 1992)
- Analyzes antebellum southern women writers' responses to Stowe

Marianne Noble, *The Masochistic Pleasures of Sentimental Literature* (Princeton: Princeton University Press, 2000)
- Argues that scenes of black suffering in *Uncle Tom's Cabin* would actually have given some readers a perverse pleasure linked to masochistic desire; explains how this dimension of the novel's appeal undercut its spiritual agenda (by objectifying the suffering of slaves) while still playing into its political goals (by making the suffering of slaves accessible to white [women] readers through these potentially erotic channels)

Timothy Powell, *Ruthless Democracy: A Multicultural Interpretation of the American Renaissance* (Princeton: Princeton University Press, 2000)
- Positions *Uncle Tom's Cabin* in relation to several African-American writers and to the African colonization movement

Stephen Railton, *Authorship and Audience: Literary Performance in the American Renaissance* (Princeton: Princeton University Press, 1991)
- Considers *Uncle Tom's Cabin* as one of many nineteenth-century texts constructing American authorship as a social performance; characterizes Stowe's novel as both progressive and conventional, so that the book could present a controversial argument about slavery and draw a huge audience

Ishmael Reed, *Flight to Canada* (New York: Random House, 1976)
- Parodies *Uncle Tom's Cabin* and satirizes Stowe herself to critique her misappropriation of African American culture

Arthur Riss, "Racial Essentialism and Family Values in Uncle Tom's Cabin," *American Quarterly* 46 (1994): 513–44.
- Points out how Stowe invoked views of blacks' supposedly inherent race-based traits to argue that they were "naturally" drawn to Christianity and therefore worthy of being treated with humanity; provides an historically situated view of many whites' attitudes toward racial differences in Stowe's day

Sarah Robbins, *Managing Literacy, Mothering America: Women's Narratives on Reading and Writing in the Nineteenth Century* (Pittsburgh: University of Pittsburgh Press, 2004)
- Interprets *Uncle Tom's Cabin* and Stowe's career within the context of her writing domestic literacy narratives; highlights links between Stowe's and Frances Harper's writings on slavery

Lora Romero, *Home Fronts: Domesticity and its Critics in the Antebellum United States* (Durham: Duke University Press, 1997)
- Includes an insightful chapter on *Uncle Tom's Cabin* as "Bio-political Resistance" that conflates the patriarchal oppression of women with slavery's oppression of blacks

Debra J. Rosenthal, *A Routledge Literary Sourcebook on Harriet Beecher Stowe's "Uncle Tom's Cabin"* (New York: Routledge, 2004)
- Reprints key excerpts from *Uncle Tom's Cabin* and from secondary criticism of the novel; offers a concise overview of Stowe's life

Karen Sanchez-Eppler, *Touching Liberty: Abolition, Feminism, and the Politics of the Body* (Berkeley: University of California Press, 1993)
- Re-reads sentimental anti-slavery writing, including Stowe's work, to highlight how white authors sometimes used this discourse to write about anxieties they could not voice directly; points out ways in which nineteenth-century proto-feminism and abolitionism could appropriate and displace the black body

Susan Belasco Smith, "Serialization and the Nature of *Uncle Tom's Cabin*," in *Periodical Literature in Nineteenth-Century America*, edited by Kenneth M. Price and Susan Belasco Smith (Charlottesville: University Press of Virginia, 1995), pp. 69–89
- Examines the impact of its *National Era* periodical venue on the initial publication of *Uncle Tom's Cabin*

Eric J. Sundquist, ed., *New Essays on Uncle Tom's Cabin* (Cambridge: Cambridge University Press, 1986)
- Presents influential essays bringing race, gender, genre, and other interpretive lenses to bear on *Uncle Tom's Cabin*; includes scholarship by Richard Yarborough, Jean Yellin, Karen Halttunen, Robert Stepto, and Elizabeth Ammons

Jane Tompkins, *Sensational Designs: The Cultural Work of American Fiction 1790–1860* (New York: Oxford University Press, 1985)
- Critiques the traditional canon's devaluing of works like *Uncle Tom's Cabin*; describes the features of Stowe's work that exercised sentimental power in her day

Cindy Weinstein, ed., *The Cambridge Companion to Harriet Beecher Stowe* (Cambridge: Cambridge University Press, 2004)
- Assembles a wide range of scholarship on Stowe, such as new work on texts other than *Uncle Tom's Cabin*; includes essays by Samuel Otter, Michael T. Gilmore, Gillian Brown, Audrey Fisch, Judie Newman, Marjorie Pryse, Gregg Crane, Ronald G. Walters, Lawrence Buell, Carolyn L. Karcher, and Kenneth W. Warren

Laura Wexler, *Tender Violence: Domestic Visions in an Age of US Imperialism* (Chapel Hill: University of North Carolina Press, 2000)

- Reconsiders Ann Douglas's and Jane Tompkins's scholarship on Stowe in the context of a larger project critiquing the imperial dimensions of sentimental culture

Linda Williams, *Playing the Race Card: Melodramas of Black and White from Uncle Tom to O. J. Simpson* (Princeton: Princeton University Press, 2001)
- Identifies ways that *Uncle Tom's Cabin* contributed to an ideology and associated representations of black males as victims and also as brutes in American melodramas

Cynthia Griffin Wolff, "'Masculinity' in *Uncle Tom's Cabin*," *American Quarterly* 47 (1995), 595–618.
- Highlights an antebellum movement to promote a Christian, caring version of masculinity consistent with Stowe's characterization of her title character, thereby suggesting that his (seeming) passivity would actually have been viewed positively by many readers of her day

Elizabeth Young, *Disarming the Nation: Women's Writing and the American Civil War* (Chicago: University of Chicago Press, 1999)
- Sets *Uncle Tom's Cabin* in context with other women's Civil War texts, ranging from familiar authors such as Louisa May Alcott, Frances Harper and Margaret Mitchell to memoirists Loreta Velazquez and Elizabeth Keckley

Electronic resources

http://www.iath.virginia.edu/utc/
Uncle Tom's Cabin and American Culture is a rich and wide-ranging Web site whose resources include numerous illustrations from various editions of the novel

http://www.scribblingwomen.org/hbscassy.htm
On the "Scribbling Women" Web site, a project of the Public Media Foundation at Northeastern University, hear a dramatization of "Cassy" (an excerpt from *Uncle Tom's Cabin*) and survey lesson plans for studying the novel

http://xroads.virginia.edu/HYPER/STOWE/stowe.html
An electronic copy of *Uncle Tom's Cabin*, along with critical resources, is available on the University of Virginia's Web site of primary texts in American literature

http://www.harrietbeecherstowecenter.org/index_home.shtml
The author's home in Hartford is the location of the Harriet Beecher Stowe Center, a library and public history organization whose Web site provides diverse resources

Index

Note: Because the characters in Stowe's writing, particularly in *Uncle Tom's Cabin*, are often referenced (only) by first name, they are alphabetized here accordingly, e.g., "Eliza Harris" rather than "Harris, Eliza," with the exceptions being Mrs Shelby and Senator and Mrs Bird. Harriet Beecher Stowe is designated as HBS and *Uncle Tom's Cabin* as *UTC*. Characters from *UTC* have individual entries; characters from other works are listed under their respective titles

housekeeping 10. *See* also *American Women's Home, Hearth and Home, House and Home Papers*

I Ain't Yo' Uncle 81–82; Stowe in 81–82; Tom in 81–82; Topsy in 81–82. *See* also Alexander, Robert; *UTC*, dramatizations of
Incidents in the Life of a Slave Girl 109–10
internationalization of Stowe 122
Iola Leroy 111
Italy 85, 86. *See* also *Agnes of Sorrento*

Jacobs, Harriet (Linda Brent) 109–10, 112
Jewett, John 7, 57–60; negotiations with 58
Johnson, Charles 123
Jones, Jacqueline 20
Julius, Uncle (in Charles Chesnutt's writing) 47–48
Jungle, The, influence of *UTC* on 97–98

Key to "Uncle Tom's Cabin", A 23, 54, 58, 61–66, 90, 96, 97, 105, 122; defense of *UTC* 61, 100, 101; meaning of title's metaphor 62; religion in 23; research approaches 108, 110; southern characters in 102
Kindred 112

Lady Byron Vindicated 11, 15, 95–96, 97
Lane Theological Seminary 4, 5, 6
Legree, Simon *See* Simon Legree
Leopard's Spots, The 103
letter writing 24
Liberator, The 20, 33
Liberia 40–43
Lincoln, Abraham 2
Litchfield Academy 3

literary marketplace, women's place and Stowe's place in 17, 122

Maine 6, 7, 32, 34
Mandarin 10–11, 87–89. *See* also Florida, *Palmetto Leaves*; travel writing
Marie St Clare 55, 102
Martineau, Harriet 24, 72, 85, 121
masculinity, black; masculinity, Christian. *See UTC*, masculinity and black masculinity in
material culture and *UTC* 99
May, Georgiana 4, 5, 6, 11
Mayflower, The 5, 29–30, 58
McCray, Florine Thayer 1
McIntosh, Maria 100, 101
Meer, Sarah 46, 75
Melville, Herman 117, 119
Men of Our Times 19
middle class – Beecher family's place in 24; gender roles in 13–16; women in 49
Minister's Wooing, The 10, 85, 91–92; Aaron Burr 92; connections to Catharine and Lyman Beecher 92; critique of Calvinism 23; James Marvyn 92; Mary Scudder 91–92; Samuel Hopkins 91–92
Minnie's Sacrifice 110
minstrelsy 21, 44–47, 77, 79. *See* also blackface in *UTC*; Meer, Sarah; *UTC*, minstrelsy in
Mitchell, Margaret 104
moral suasion 15, 56
Morrison, Toni 107, 112, 113
mulatta/o characters in *UTC* 56. *See* also Eliza Harris; George Harris
My Wife and I 96

Native Son 112, 120
National Era 7, 17, 18, 21, 30, 33, 41, 49, 53, 57, 76
New Criticism 117

*"Uncle Tom's Cabin" Contrasted with
Buckingham Hall The Planter's
Home* 101, 102
Uncle Tom's Children 112

Washington, Booker T. 112, 113
We and Our Neighbors 96
Webb, Mary 74–76. *See* also *The
Christian Slave*
Williams, Linda 45, 81
Williams, Sherley Anne 112
Wilson, Forrest 122
Woodhull, Victoria 15
works of HBS *See* individual listings
for these titles: *Agnes of Sorrento,
American Women's Home, The
Christian Slave, Dred, Footsteps of
the Master,* "The Freeman's
Dream," *Hearth and Home, House
and Home Papers, A Key to* Uncle
Tom's Cabin, *Lady Byron
Vindicated, The Mayflower, Men
of Our Times, The Minister's
Wooing, My Wife and I, Oldtown
Folks, Palmetto Leaves, The Pearl
of Orr's Island, Pink and White
Tyranny, Poganuc People, Sunny
Memories of Foreign Lands,* "The
True Story of Lady Byron's Life,"
"Uncle Lot," *Uncle Tom's Cabin,
We and Our Neighbors*
Wright, Richard 56, 60, 112, 113,
120

Yarborough, Richard 111
Yellin, Jean 109, 122, 132

Zagarell, Sandra 28